# And Is It True?

## TRUTH, GOD A
## NO-MAN'S LA

And is it true? And is it true
This most tremendous tale of all.

*'Christmas' by John Betjeman*

*For*
*Nicholas and Lindsey*

*Richard Clarke*

# And Is It True?

## TRUTH, GOD AND NO-MAN'S LAND

DOMINICAN PUBLICATIONS

First published (2000) by
Dominican Publications
42 Parnell Square
Dublin 1

ISBN 1-871552-75-3

British Library Cataloguing in Publications Data.
A catalogue record for this book is available
from the British Library.

Cover design by Bill Bolger

Printed in Ireland by
ColourBooks, Baldoyle, Dublin 13

*Copyright Acknowledgements*
The author and publishers are grateful to those who gave
permission to reproduce copyright material. While every effort
has been made to trace the holder of copyright in texts quoted,
the publishers apologise if any case has been overlooked, and if
an oversight comes to their attention will make good the
omission in any subsequent edition.

# Contents

# Acknowledgements

Many people, over many years, and in many different settings, have contributed to the thinking behind this book. I thank them all and hope that some of them will recognise their involvement in my spiritual journeyings.

I would wish to express my gratitude also to Peter Francis and the staff of St Deiniol's Library in Hawarden (where much of this was written) for their helpfulness and jovial hospitality, and to the clergy of the Dioceses of Meath and Kildare (on whom, from time to time, sections of this book have been 'tried out') for their continuing patience.

Finally, may I thank sincerely my secretary Karen Seaman for her cheerful willingness to decipher the indecipherable, my friend Bernard Treacy for encouraging me to believe that this book should be written, and my wife Linda for encouraging me to believe that it could be written.

# Pre-text

This may be one of those occasions when the dedication of a book explains much of its purpose. Nicholas and Lindsey are my children, but children now only in the genetic sense. I will not embarrass them further, beyond saying that they are interesting and intelligent young adults, and I want them to understand what makes me think the things I think, and do the things I do.

This is therefore not so much a piece of Christian apologetic as a more personal *apologia*, and it is in consequence far from a systematic theology in either the technical or the colloquial sense. It makes no claims to originality and might indeed best be described as a series of musings on the business of searching for faith with integrity, but an integrity that I hope encompasses both a ruthless honesty and also a wholeness of being that seeks to leave no place for compartmentalisation within the self.

As will probably become evident in the course of the book, this pursuit also draws heavily (even if at times somewhat subliminally) on the thought of a number of writers who might genuinely be said to have haunted me over many years, in particular Albert Camus, Wilfrid Owen, Simone Weil and Miguel de Unamuno. Although somewhat disparate as a group, there is perhaps a common golden thread running through the creative writing of all of them. In the first place, each of them was unquestionably passionate in his or her search for meaning, and equally heedless of the consequences. Secondly, I would take to be almost axiomatic the conviction of Emerson that one may have either truth or repose, but one may not have both. And this restlessness for truth is also something which these writers share together. The passion and the restlessness are things I would wish my children to share.

I also hold (as a rather obvious corollary to Emerson's epigram) that neither truth nor God may be found in what we might call entrenched positions. Much of what I wish to say on the matter therefore revolves around the image of no-man's land. I have, however, come to realise (rather to my surprise) that this picture of no-man's land, despite a renewed interest over the past few years in the First World War, may no longer be one that supports itself without some further explanation.

No-man's land, in the military terms of that war, was the place between the lines of trenches, into which soldiers had to move if they were to advance. But it was also a place of acute vulnerability, a place where one is exposed, almost defence-less, often floundering, probably wounded, and very likely caught in continuing cross-fire from the trenches on both sides. It was a place of fear but also the only place from which any advance could proceed.

I happen to believe that real truth, even the truth of God, is something that can never be entrenched, for all that it must (if it is indeed truth) relate in some way to some concept of objectivity. But it will very often be distantly 'out there' in the vulnerability and insecurity of no-man's land. I am certain that we should not expect to find truth or God in the safety of our personal custom-built trenches.

The suggestion I am making throughout this book is that a metaphorical no-man's land between the certainties of entrenchment is, for many people, the only place where integrity is possible and where the God of the Christian vision may 'in truth' be encountered. It was Simone Weil who remarked in one of her *Notebooks*:

> The soul's attitude towards God is not a thing to be verified by the soul itself, because God is elsewhere, in heaven, in secret. If one thinks to have verified it, this is

really some earthly thing, masquerading under the label of God.[1]

The need to seek for an objective truth that is lurking somewhere, however indistinctly, behind faith is, I am certain, profoundly important for many people. This is so even in the midst of a *fin de siècle* post-modernism which prevails today and would query the meaning of all language and human discourse. The idea of God has somehow to be more than a mere word-game for people, as they stagger in the slime and fear of daily existence, searching for either faith or God, or for both, wondering whether what the poet Philip Larkin calls 'our almost-instinct' might possibly be almost true.[2]

And so the *idée fixe* which gives a pattern to these reflections is derived primarily from an engagement that is pastoral rather than intellectual. In short, what follows could only have been written as a direct response to encounters within pastoral ministry. Although there will be little or no anecdote, what is to be explored nevertheless emerges directly from witnessing and sometimes sharing the frustrations, sufferings and stumbling of men, women and children who almost miraculously kept within range of faith, albeit in a no-man's land of anxiety and uncertainty. And they did not walk in this place because Christianity was good for them or working well for them, which it most certainly was not at that moment in their lives. Indeed, they may well have been enduring spiritual agony and disillusionment but yet they felt, often reluctantly and probably only 'on balance', that there was some connection between themselves and a truth beyond, or even just something beyond, and, ultimately, this was really what mattered. Nor were these decisions to hang on to the instincts of

1. Simone Weil, *First and Last Notebooks*, trans. Richard Rees, 1970, Oxford, Oxford University Press, p. 145.
2. 'An Arundel Tomb', Philip Larkin, *Collected Poems*, 1988, London, The Marvell Press, and Faber and Faber.

faith characterised by either complaisance or fatalism; more often than not, they were actions of sublime courage.

The underlying conviction behind what much of what I want to express may consequently be summarised in this single observation: if people can somehow believe that there is something true behind what Christianity proclaims, and that there is a connection between the self and some structure which is beyond or above the purely human experience of reality, they may well overlook the obvious foibles or repulsiveness of the visible Church which they can see only too clearly, and may even forgive the perceived indifference or savagery of the invisible God in whom they do not even wish to believe. Whether Christianity is attractive or even whether it is workable then becomes a secondary consideration. In her poem *Ego*, Stevie Smith poses the question

> What care I, if good God be,
> If he be not good to me?[3]

Many people do, strangely, still cling, however angrily or reluctantly, to a God who is not good to them, if they can somehow manage to believe in his objective existence. But they will not believe in God as the cosmic genie, a role which for much of the time he does not even seem after all to achieve particularly effectively. Nor do they believe in him (and this is probably of more significance) because of any great fear of the logical consequences of his non-existence – the conclusion that death is a full stop on an individual's existence. Indeed God's non-existence might, at a particular point of pain or disillusionment, be almost preferable to his existence.

The whole conundrum was neatly focussed for me recently when a Methodist minister based in London told of a teenager in a church youth club who had asked him the stark question

---

3. Stevie Smith, *Selected Poems*, ed. James MacGibbon, 1978, Harmondsworth, Penguin Books.

'Are you a vicar because you think it's true, or because you think it's good for you?' The dichotomy at the heart of Christian thinking today can hardly have been more incisively exposed. I have no doubt that I am a believer and a priest because I believe that the prospect of truth is of more importance than the plausibility of benefits.

# 1

## Only Connecting

E. M. Forster's novel *Howard's End* begins with the famous compact epigraph, 'Only Connect'. Within the novel, this concerns the making of connections (albeit with little hope of success) between the prosaic and the passionate, the rural with the suburban, between the intellectual and the commercial. It does not seem fanciful to suggest that there might also be a connecting of individual occurrences with a greater significance that lies behind them. Not perhaps for Forster, but that phrase, 'only connect', has also a profoundly religious application.

Religion is etymologically about connecting with something beyond the self. In an earlier cultural context in western society, religion as a connecting with God was a relatively straightforward matter for most individuals or for society at large. It was not that people were then not as good at thinking or at exploring as their descendants, but rather that a structure of faith was fundamental to the entire culture. This has long since changed. Matthew Arnold's poem of the 1860s, *Dover Beach*,[1] has been much plundered for its remarkable imagery of a society where the culture of faith is patently in decline.

> The Sea of Faith
> Was once, too, at the full, and round earth's shore
> Lay like the folds of a bright girdle furl'd.
> But now I only hear
> Its melancholy, long withdrawing roar,
> Retreating, to the breath
> Of the night wind.

---

1. *Victorian Poetry*, 1996, Harmondsworth, Penguin Books.

Even the phrase 'the Sea of Faith' has been famously appropriated (albeit with scant regard for the original context) for what is in every sense a peculiarly Anglican postmodernist encounter with a non-real deity. Whatever for that, Arnold's bleak imagery of the retreat of religious faith is not one which can be seriously gainsaid from the perspective of western society a century and a half after the lines were written. The erosion of an undergirding culture of religious faith is a fact of life, dismaying for some and a source of contentment for others.

But it is perhaps the image of the beach itself that is more properly relevant to an exploration of truth and faith. And it is when we move to the next and final stanza in Arnold's poem that the personal implications of being on the beach, when the sea of faith has retreated, become evident. Speaking to his wife 'Flu' on their honeymoon (it is generally believed), Arnold continues,

> Ah, love, let us be true
> To one another! For the world, which seems
> To lie before us like a land of dreams,
> So various, so beautiful, so new,
> Hath really neither joy, nor love, nor light,
> Nor certitude, nor peace, nor help for pain …

In other words, there is for Arnold no connection between what people feel for one another, or think about one another, or apprehend as good, and a world that is in reality totally neutral with merely the illusory appearance of beauty and light. This is a significant point of departure for discourse on faith. At heart, it is the question as to whether Arnold's sense of love for Flu was simply a particular conjunction of neurones without further significance (except of course for what Arnold himself felt he was feeling), or whether it fits within a larger edifice where love has a context beyond the individual's perception of it.

Many, even in Arnold's day, would have had no doubts on the matter. Scientifically, we may describe human behaviour and even human emotions in purely mechanical terms. Physiologically, it may certainly be predicated that our hopes and fears, our feelings or ambitions, are in fact the infinitely complex dances of a vast collection of nerve cells and associated molecules. And this standpoint is now being reinforced from the opposite direction: in 'biobotics' it has recently proved possible to produce what are termed *cyberinsects*, electronic versions of crickets or ants which can simulate the patterns of neurone signalling found in their living counterparts, so that the cyberinsect will respond 'instinctively' to stimuli in exactly the same behavioural patterns as these counterparts.

Scientists often wish to add that the behavioural patterns of neurones and nerve cells are in fact all that our emotions and feelings add up to, these and nothing more. And this has often been the place where science and religion cease to dialogue. The defender of religion will retort that, in saying that our hopes or beliefs are nothing more than the behaviour of neurones, the scientist has (without admitting it) veered out of the area of science into the field of philosophy. The scientist will suggest that by loading a structure of metaphysics on top of physics, the defender of religion has gratuitously and fraudulently added a superstructure where there was no logical need to do so. The simple fact is that neither is even beginning to communicate with the other.

And this particular discussion has inevitably been given a new dimension with the rise of deconstructionism in recent decades. This approach to philosophy sets itself to 'deconstruct' those modes of thought and language that have been fashioned by a traditional cultural assumption that there is a connection between ordinary events or feelings and a reality or truth beyond them; inevitably it will draw the conclusion that there can be no such connection.

We may probably proceed very little further before ad-
dressing the fundamental question of what is meant by truth.
It was a question in which Pontius Pilate found a useful escape
route, and it has a long history of being elusive. But the
question lies at the very centre of all post-structuralist exploration and discourse, which would argue that by defining
truth we are, in that action of defining, creating our own
template of truth. Hence any definition of truth is, literally, by
definition circular.

Truth has, after all, at least two contexts. There is, first, the
epistemological sense. This concerns the relationship between the mind and the appropriation of what it discerns as
truth. And then there is a more extended, metaphysical
context in the objective reality (if indeed it is objective) that
our mind seeks to appropriate.

At this stage there may be some value in introducing the
rather eccentric figure of Manuel de Unamuno into the
discussion. He does not provide a ready riposte to either a
deconstructionist or to a wholly mechanistic view of existence,
but he does bring a certain passion to the pursuit of truth.
Unamuno, to place him into some context, was a Basque
intellectual born in 1864 who, for most of his seventy-two
years, fought with almost everybody and everything around
him. He was a Professor of Greek (in Salamanca), a novelist,
poet, dramatist, and a rather unsystematic existentialist philosopher. As a liberal opponent of the Spanish monarchy, he
was exiled from Spain for much of the 1920s. He abandoned
the Catholic faith at a young age and, in direct response, his
books were placed on the *Index* for the remainder of its
existence. Unamuno also had an extraordinary fear of death,
however, and he would freely admit that he needed to believe
in God in order that his personal immortality might remain at
least a reasonable hope.

There are therefore passages in his writings where many would wish to part company from him, particularly from those places where he skates unto distinctly thin ice over some irrational and almost pitiable wish-fulfilment. But there is far more to Unamuno than that.

In an essay entitled 'What is truth?' [2] he attacks with gusto the aphorism of Voltaire that if God did not exist it would have been necessary to have invented him. Unamuno retorts that an invented God would be a commodity of venal dishonesty for oneself and for others, and 'would not even be a non-God, but would be an anti-God, an absolute Devil.' After a characteristically scorching attack on what he sees as the 'vulgarity, imbecility and dotage' of much traditional Catholic Thomist philosophy, he then goes on to admit that what a Thomist would call moral truth, as distinct from metaphysical truth, is probably the only real truth, 'the radical truth'. He defines this as a conformity between external language and internal judgement. What is implied here of course is that language may indeed at least attempt to express more than that which humanity may verify empirically, or may choose to invent.

Here we step ineluctably back into the world of linguistic philosophy. What is called (albeit with some generalisation) logical positivism would instantly take issue with Unamuno, and maintain that the only proper use for language is for whatever may be verified empirically or logically. And there is no doubt that logical positivism, for all that it may be regarded by many as *passé*, still has a profound influence on the way in which much religious discussion today is conducted. But is this necessary? Central to the thought of Ludwig Wittgenstein, who is usually credited as being the foundation stone for modern linguistic philosophy, was the insight that the most

2.  Miguel de Unamuno, *The Agony of Christianity and Essays on Faith.* trans. Anthony Kerrigan, 1974, London, Routledge and Kegan Paul 'What is truth?', pp. 165-184

significant things of all cannot be stated by language but, at best indicated by our use of words. He would have wished us to keep silent on the things that really matter. But the realisation that language is not the best vehicle for such discourse surely does not discount the importance of attempting the discourse? Language is after all, the only vehicle we have.

And so, for the purposes of these reflections, it may be sufficient to say that in what follows, truth may be understood as having to do with what is extrinsic connecting with what is intrinsic, and what is objective connecting with what is subjective. In more traditional philosophical categories, we might speak of a ground between the purely empirical and the purely rational. For the empiricist, knowledge of the world is conveyed to a mind which is, in effect, a blank piece of paper. For the rationalist, an understanding of the world is deduced from ideas and structures which are innate in the mind. In other words, we may seek to relate experience to what our mind can make of it (the empirical), or we may use our minds as the primary instrument and relate this mind to what is outside it, if anything (the rational).

Yet, at the end of all our philosophising, we can never be absolutely sure that there is anything coherent beyond ourselves or even that we ourselves are coherent. Any order we put on anything (whether from an entirely rationalist or an entirely empirical perspective) may be an hallucination for all that we could ever establish objectively. Both extremes, in their absolute forms – the supposedly totally empirical or totally rationalist, the supposedly wholly objective or the supposedly wholly subjective – are inherently sterile if not self-contradictory. Belief is surely beached, and with the same tragic consequences as for a whale. There must be a connection between the empirical and the rationalist, if we are to not to remain beached eternally.

It is the ground between the tidinesses of unsullied empiricism and equally unsullied rationalism, or between those parallel certainties of non-structure and structure, that we may find the only place for movement or advance, or 'radical truth'. This *ground between* can never be a comfortable place. It is a philosophical no-man's land.

On a different axis, the *ground between* was, for the great French writer and philosopher, Albert Camus, the place of the *absurd*. It is unfortunate that this term 'absurd', because it is so much part of everyday language, almost lends itself to trivialisation. In Camus' usage it is far from trivial. Writing from the standpoint of one who assumes the absence of any over-arching structure beyond or above human existence, Camus nevertheless finds an absurdity, not in the absence of meaning, but in the confrontation between the sense of the irrationality and the meaninglessness of existence, and the deep-seated human demand for clarity and ultimate purpose. For Camus, it was only when we learn to live with this absurdity and dislocation that we can cease to be alienated from our own lives and can actually move forward. Otherwise we are actors on a stage playing a part we have not learnt and do not know.

But to speak, as I would wish to do, of a Christian vision of God or of truth as a way to find a role on the stage for humanity, is to create a further layer of discomfort. Because, whether we like it or not, there can be no disembodied or abstract Christian vision of God or truth. The very essence of the Christian faith is that it incarnational, rooted in human experience. Precisely because it is so, it is people playing a role – the Church in its widest sense – who mediate and interpret the messages and signals of Christianity. Whether Church in this sense is represented by a parent, a friend, a Sunday School teacher or a passing evangelist, the Christian vision is inevitably filtered, interpreted, even distorted *en route*, but always mediated, regardless of whether the message is itself truth, fiction or fable. It is of course theoretically possible to predicate an individual, knowing nothing of the Church or any of its manifestations (or through any of its representatives), picking up a Bible, reading it from cover to cover, evaluating its claims without reference either to a commentary or to any other agency of the Christian community, and then turning this evaluation into a personal *credo*. Even if we were to allow the possibility of such an occurrence, we would still have to peel this particular onion a little further and recall that the Bible is itself the mediation and interpretation of a message by a community. There is no extrinsic truth, and certainly not a Christian truth, that has not been filtered in the course of transmission.

And so, although all radical truth and any religious truth is inevitably interpreted and distorted in the course of transmission, I begin from a supposition that there is at least the possibility of a *something somewhere*, however manipulated or strangulated it may be, that nevertheless has a reality independent of us, and that may be termed 'truth', and to which we may also connect. This possibility is not to be automatically equated with the necessary existence of God but provides what is at least a starting point for considering the possibility of God.

But given that some idea of an extrinsic objective truth, a real 'connection' between humanity and a structure of eternity, must also surely lie behind the Christian Gospel if it is to carry conviction, it is strange indeed that most of the efforts of the Christian community have been, not to proclaim a truth of connection that lies behind the unwholesome spectacle that the Church presents to the world, but instead to confront the world with what must surely be a secondary consideration, whether Christianity actually 'works'? And this concern as to whether it all 'works' is manifested pastorally, liturgically and intellectually. The need for the Church to be seen as caring and compassionate is not only a symptom of life in an age where the motto of that new and unlikeable species, the spin-doctor, is that perception is more important than reality, but it is also a genuine and altruistic wish to live up to the reputation that the Church ought to have, if it is to demonstrate that Christianity actually works.

Similarly, in every tradition of Christian community, much effort is put into the provision of worship which has immediacy and an impact. In other words, worship must be presented in such a way that it can be seen to work. And, on a purely intellectual level, it would seem that a great deal of the post-modernist debate within the Christian ambit is assuredly not about an objective truth or reality behind Christian formulations, but whether those formulations may be a useful cipher for living out a humane and satisfying existence on earth. We may thus restrict 'God' to the specifically religious dimension of human life and cage him there, where (not having any objective existence) he may do no harm and may even do us some good.

A dichotomy in religious exploration between 'whether it is true' and 'whether it works' may well be resolved within the personal experience of an individual believer (and sometimes with no sense of dislocation whatsoever), but the resolution as to whether truth or workability has the priority must always be crucial. We may argue (and, indeed, must argue) that if the Gospel is true in content but malevolent in its application, its intrinsic truth gives no grounds for conscientious adherence to its tenets. But the inherent morality or lack of morality of Christianity is not what establishes its truth. The poet A.E. Housman, an atheist as it happens, railed against 'whatever brute and blackguard made the world'.[3] But any

3. Last Poems IX. *The Works of A.E Housman*, 1994, London, Wordsworth Editions.

consideration as to whether God is indeed good or bad must always be secondary to questions as to whether he exists, and whether he is God. We might not believe that he was worthy of our praise or adoration, but we are still left with an important decision as to whether the truth of the matter is not prior to its goodness or its workability.

Truth and workability need not necessarily co-adhere. Things may indeed work for a considerable time, without being based on sound or coherent principles. As a generation of Italians discovered under Mussolini, trains may run on time for many years under a system which was not only immoral but which is also inherently contradictory. Similarly, people may be kind and generous to one another, worship may still be performed with enormous panache and choreographic impact, theologians may still find real value in a 'created God', but if some notions of objectivity, reality, and objective truth to which we connect are not at the heart of religious discourse, then we should surely remain obdurately silent in the dark.

What is certain is that we will not imprison the wholeness of truth or reality in the existence we have in a life on earth. Camus speaks of a 'nostalgia for unity', the insistence of the individual for clarity in grasping the meaning of his or her existence. But, as he points out,

> Understanding the world for a man is reducing it to the human, stamping it with his seal. The cat's universe is not the universe of the ant-hill. The truism 'All thought is anthropomorphic' has no other meaning.[4]

When we seek to stretch the limits of our anthropomorphic thoughts, we will inevitably be on vulnerable ground, a no-man's land, perhaps even that place to which Arnold brings us at the conclusion of *Dover Beach*,

---

4. Albert Camus, *The Myth of Sisyphus*. trans Justin O'Brien, 1975, Harmondsworth, Penguin Books, p. 23.

Swept by confused alarms of struggle and flight,
Where ignorant armies clash by night.

It is of course possible to withdraw from the arena of struggle entirely and fall back on what is almost the total mirror-image of the post-modernist faith in a non-real God. This is the approach of fideism, which says in effect that an individual may just know that God is there and may know what to believe about him, because faith comes directly from God's grace and not through anything else (notably reason or observation) that might actually help to convince the individual. A faith which is intuited directly (and without the struggles of no-man's land) has the undoubted advantage that no-one may deny it on grounds of logic because, when all is said and done, we are not actually 'inside' any other person. It is however, without question, a spiritual trench (if not a bunker), and certainly it is a position from which no useful movement is possible.

If an individual relationship with God – which by its nature cannot and need not be subjected to the questioning of others – is all that there is to faith, then we are in no position to convince anyone else nor should we attempt to do so. An individual's faith cannot be denied, but neither may it be validly communicated to others. It is also difficult to see how a God who is utterly individualistic in self-disclosure could be anything other than a concept rather than a reality of any kind. It was Unamuno who once observed that to believe in God, but without passion or doubt or even at times without despair, is not to believe in God, but to believe only in the idea of God.

# 2

# Truth in No-Man's Land

Even for those who were born generations after the First World War, the trenches of Flanders and the Somme can still exercise a strong fascination. It may be in part the sheer scale of the carnage, the apparent helplessness of good men on both sides of the conflict to see the futility of it all, or the fact that a strange beauty is still be found in the heroism, in the protest, and most certainly in the poetry of the Great War. Perhaps we now see also that the trenches of that war represent as much an arena of cosmic encounter between truth and untruth, as a temporal battleground of blood and fear between soldiers of different nations. It is certainly not that truth was firmly in one of the trenches and absent from the other. Far from it. Both sides may indeed have believed that they had gone to war for righteousness. Church leaders joined forces with politicians to encourage them to believe so. The verdict of history is otherwise.

The metaphor of no-man's land provides a particularly appropriate image in this context for the struggle between faith and non-faith, and the ultimate quest for truth. Many of those about to die in the trenches of the First World War wished to salute neither Kaiser nor King before they went 'over the top'. The glory of sacrifice for King and Country was a powerful emotion for those at home (and it may well have brought real comfort to those who were bereaved by the carnage of the Somme or Passchendale) but at the front, things were different. The poets had their minds on things more subversive than patriotic rhetoric. As Osbert Sitwell expressed it, with an insolent savagery,

> You hope that we shall tell you that they found their happiness in fighting,

Or that they died with a song on their lips,
Or that we shall use the old familiar phrases
With which your paid servants please you in the Press:
But we are poets
And shall tell the truth.[1]

And the minds of those who thought at all (and not just the poets, it should be said), as they awaited death or mutilation for themselves, were often concentrated on the most fundamental question of all, as to whether there was a God or, at any rate, a God worth believing in. What is of particular interest is the ambiguity of belief in some of those who waited for death. This strange ambiguity not only has a fascination in itself, but it is also of value in seeking to grasp the point that truth and God cannot be entrenched, if the search for either truth or God is to be anything more than word-play.

In the trenches of the 1914-18 War, there were those who had rejected the formal Christian faith, but who nevertheless were unable to remove the language of God from their thought and writings; equally, there were those who had retained their Christian faith, but who wrote in a cold stoicism that was clearly at odds with the basic tenets of Christianity. Herein there was a definite no-man's land between belief and non-belief, a place where many today, who may be far removed from the blood and death of the trenches of history, might find their only home – uncomfortable and vulnerable though it may be.

But to return to the reality of the First World War, we may consider, as a paradigm of this creative tension and ambiguity of non-faith and faith, two of the finest poets that war gave to posterity, Wilfrid Owen and Charles Hamilton Sorley.

Wilfrid Owen, who used the famous phrase of 'finding God in no-man's land' in a letter to his mother in 1917, had

1. 'Rhapsode'. *Poetry of the Great War*, ed. Dominic Hibberd and John Onions, 1986, London, Macmillan.

rejected the Christian faith long before the Great War began.[2] Coming from an evangelical background, and intending to be ordained (or, as seems more likely, 'intended for ordination' by his mother), Owen spent a year in the parish of Dunsden to work as an unpaid assistant with the vicar as preparation prior to training for ordination. Here he developed a virulent dislike of evangelicalism, which he saw as obsessive and a form of 'soul-suicide'. Owen certainly repudiated orthodox religious faith at this stage, and probably rejected Christian belief of any kind. Yet, for all his progression away from religious belief, Owen's poetry remains full of biblical imagery, some openly ironic but some intensely and almost unbearably poignant in its departure from faith. A stanza from his poem *Exposure* serves as example:

> Since we believe not otherwise can kind fires burn;
> Nor ever suns smile true on child, or field, or fruit.
> For God's invincible spring our love is made afraid;
> Therefore, not loath, we lie out here, therefore were born,
> For love of God seems dying.[3]

There is a more famous line from his poetry that also seems to stretch out towards a retreating God – 'I too saw God through mud – The mud that cracked on cheeks when wretches smiled ... '[4]

But we can of course counter this with Owen's strong sense of futility. In the poem of that title, he points to meaninglessness, as he reflects on the death of a soldier, that even the 'kind old sun' cannot wake, as once it could wake him at home or 'even in France' –

2. On Owen's life and thought see Dominic Hibberd, *Owen the Poet*, 1986, London, Macmillan.
3. *The Penguin Book of First World War Poetry*, ed. Jon Silkin, 1979, Harmondsworth, Penguin Books.
4. 'Apologia Pro Poemate Meo'. *The Penguin Book of First World War Poetry*.

Was it for this the clay grew tall?
– O what made fatuous sunbeams toil
To break earth's sleep at all? [5]

It would serve no purpose to seek to 'Christianise' Owen. Indeed it would be both patronising and hypocritical. But what we may legitimately do is suggest that in Owen's strange unbelief there is an intense ambiguity, a no-man's land between a longing for faith and what is almost an *anti-faith*.

This is strongly characterised in one of his last poems, *Greater Love*. The title is a biblical allusion – 'greater love has no man than that he lay down his life for his friends … ' (Jn 15:13). Owen revised the poem several times. One particular line reads in an early draft as 'Love seems not to care' but in the final form became 'Where God seems not to care'.[6] We should not read too much into this alteration but it may well be significant that in this final year of Owen's life, he had established a friendship with Robert Ross, Oscar Wilde's most faithful friend, and there is most certainly a Wildean touch to this poem, where the cross and Christ's suffering are earthed in the failures and rejection of humans. Owen certainly knew Wilde's *De Profundis*, where Christ is the exemplar of pity and of suffering.

We could make too much of a shift in Owen's psyche in the last year of his life when it may be that for the first time he came to terms spiritually with his homosexuality, and could in consequence relate again personally to religious imagery. Certainly the last line of *Greater Love* contains a strange reference to Christ's resurrection response to Mary Magdalene, 'Woman why do you weep?' and then 'Do not touch me … ' The entire poem demonstrates an uneasy and uncertain dialogue with the relationship of men and women but also with religious belief itself.

5. 'Futility'. Ibid.
6. See Hibberd, *Owen the Poet*,. pp. 158-161

Red lips are not so red
As the stained stones kissed by the English dead.
Kindness of wooed and wooer
Seems shame to their love pure.
Love, your eyes lose lure
When I behold eyes wounded in my stead!

Your slender attitude
Trembles not exquisite like limbs knife-skewed,
Rolling and rolling there
Where God seems not to care;
Till the fierce love they bear
Cramps them in death's extreme decrepitude.

Your love sings not so soft, –
Though even as wind murmuring through raftered
    loft,–
Your dear voice is not so dear,
Gentle, and evening clear,
As theirs whom none now hear,
Now earth has stopped their piteous mouths that
    coughed.

Heart, you were never hot
Nor large, nor full like hearts made great with shot;
And though your hand be pale,
Pale are all which trail
Your cross through flame and hail;
Weep, you may weep, for you may touch them not.[7]

Owen experimented a great deal with the final part of this poem and at one stage replaced 'Your cross' with 'rifles' in the penultimate line. He must have been aware of the use being made at home of a crucifixion symbolism in defence of the War, even of the blasphemous idea of the sacrifice of British soldiers as a 'lesser Calvary' – and thus of the possible misuse

7. *Poetry of the Great War* ed. Dominic Hibberd and John Onions.

of his phraseology for purposes of propaganda.

What Owen believed or did not believe about God when he died, one week before the war ended in November 1918, can only be a matter for conjecture. What is certain is that the language and the imagery of Christianity were still part of his make-up and that for him the borders of God and no-God were not defined trenches. There was a no-man's land in his thinking where belief and non-belief could not easily be separated. Precisely because it is no-man's land, we cannot draw a line in the ground to define a border between the possession of one side or the other. This aspect of no-man's land may become clearer when we turn to the other of our chosen war poets, Charles Hamilton Sorley.

Sorley and Owen represent almost mirror-images of one another. The contrast between them has an enticing symmetry about it. Of privileged social background and public school education, Sorley died early in the War, at the Battle of Loos in 1915, aged only twenty. He had barely found a mature poetic voice, although there were those, including John Masefield, who believed that he was (potentially at least) a poet of genius.

Contrasts with Owen are of more than academic interest. Much of Owen's erudition was self-acquired; Sorley attended King's College Choir School, Marlborough, and won a scholarship to University College Oxford. Owen had a particular feeling for France, having lived there for some time before the War; Sorley, on the other hand, spent a few months in Germany before the outbreak of war, and never disavowed a considerable admiration for the country, its people and its culture. Owen, having come from a pronouncedly evangelical background, found that he had outgrown what he saw as its stultifying self-obsession; Sorley came from a traditional High Anglican family and seems to have retained at least an outward adherence to Christianity until his death.

Far from the poetry of war, Sorley before the war had written a somewhat pietistic poem, *Expectans Expectavi*, subsequently set to music by Charles Wood and still one of the classics of the established repertoire of cathedral music. The anthem contains a powerful and moving affirmation of personal spirituality which perhaps goes some distance to explaining the enduring popularity of the work, but which, in its gentle certainties, could scarcely be further removed from the harsh contemptuousness of Owen towards orthodox Christian belief:

> This sanctuary of my soul
> Unwitting I keep light and whole
> Unlatched and lit, if Thou shoulds't care
> To enter or to tarry there.

But Sorley's war poems have a bleakness and cold irony about them that suggest considerably less of a comfortable or comforting religion than would some of the struggling and probing questioning of Owen the atheist. Sorley's first cousin, the politician and academic Rab Butler, was of the belief that Sorley had never abandoned his Christian faith, and that some of his seeming cool stoicism about death was because he had no fear of dying.[8] Although Butler may be correct about Sorley's Christian beliefs remaining with him, the savagery of a poem like 'When you see millions of the mouthless dead' takes us well into a no-man's land where humanity faces the possibility that there is nothing beyond death and no significance in life on this side of death.

> When you see millions of the mouthless dead
> Across your dreams in pale battalions go,
> Say not soft things as other men have said,
> That you'll remember. For you need not so

---

8. Lord Butler, *The Art of Memory*, 1982, London, Hodder and Stoughton, pp. 113-126.

Give them not praise. For, deaf, how should they know
It is not curses heaped on each gashed head?
Nor tears. Their blind eyes see not your tears flow.
Nor honour. It is easy to be dead.
Say only this, 'They are dead.' Then add thereto,
'Yet many a better one has died before.'
Then, scanning all the o'ercrowded mass, should you
Perceive one face that you loved heretofore,
It is a spook. None wears the face you knew.
Great death has made all his for evermore.[9]

If we think of another of his poems *All the Hills and Vales along*, with its continuing theme of the soldiers marching to a return to the earth and its haunting retort, 'So be merry, so be dead', it is very difficult to discern any orthodox Christian understanding of meaning in life or of resolution beyond death.

Just as it would be patronising to claim Owen for Christianity, so, equally, it would be absurd to excommunicate Sorley. But how each responds to the torture and torments of war is significant. Sorley lets go of much traditional comfort and hope, in an engagement with nature which receives back earth, the dust of human death, not in any biblical echo of 'Dust thou art and to dust shalt thou return', but in a nihilism more of detachment than of despair. Early in the poem *All the Hills and Vales along*, Christ is placed in company with Barabbas, 'Jesus Christ and Barabbas were found the same day … ' and later, Christ's cross and Socrates' hemlock are aligned together, both born by the earth 'with joyful ease'.

Earth that blossomed and was glad
'Neath the cross that Christ had,
Shall rejoice and blossom too
When the bullet reaches you …[10]

9. *Poetry of the Great War*, ed. Dominic Hibberd and John Onions.
10. *Ibid.*

The sardonic coldness of Sorley in belief and the passion of Owen in unbelief belong together in a place where the trenches are distant. We therefore have to move on to ask: Is not this belief in the midst of unbelief, or unbelief blending with belief, in fact a necessity if we are to speak of God who is beyond the easy comprehension of humankind?

God, if he is God, cannot be a God of the black and white, of the easy certainties. If he were a God whom we can fully understand, explain or comprehend, he could not be God. And, precisely because he is a God beyond our understanding, he must also, from our human perspective, be a God in the shadows. And there will therefore be unanswered questions, there will be loose ends, there will be tangled threads that may drive us to the edge of despair.

This is not a fashionable God. People often turn to religion for comfort or for stability, and they do not want to struggle, to agonise, or even to explore. What many probably want for themselves is a consoling religion, rather than a religion that is astringent or angular in any way. And there are many people who will provide a painless religion for others, albeit on the condition that they switch off their critical faculties as soon as they step inside this religion and accept a set of absolutes and certainties without question. Sects are, almost by definition, built on absolutes. And we need to admit that for centuries the western Church was awash with a faith of absolutes. We can recognise that what we are seeing today, within many of the mainstream traditions, is a titanic confrontation between a religious absolutism on the one hand and, on the other, a questioning and exploring of faith.

We need to remember that the biblical picture is of a God who cannot be grasped with ease. In Exodus, we encounter a God who will destroy us if we seek his face directly. In the First Book of Kings, Solomon's prayer (as the ark of the covenant is brought into the Temple) is to a God who has 'chosen to live in cloud and darkness' (1 Kgs 8:12). And St Paul, not the least doctrinaire of men, wrote to the Church in Corinth that now we are seeing only 'puzzling reflections in a mirror' (1 Cor 13:12).

Most thinking, feeling people are indeed aware of the apparent absence of God at crucial times. It may begin as an intellectual concern which can quickly become an emotional anxiety and then a spiritual desperation. When we are confronted by pain or fear or confusion, in ourselves or in others, there is the instinctive cry, 'God, show yourself, and even if you will not give us the answer that we want, at least establish your presence or at very least your existence.' But there is still nothing except an opaque blankness. There is an appalling and hackneyed story of two sets of footprints on the sea-shore, representing a journey through life. For most of the journey there are two sets of footprints, representing Christ walking alongside a disciple. There is one place where there is only a single set of footprints. Looking back on the trail, the disciple complains that it was at this stage, where he was walking alone, that he most need the companionship of Christ. Christ replies that where the disciple could only see one set of footmarks they were in fact *his* footprints, and that this was because Christ was carrying the disciple. I dislike that story intensely. It is far too easy to trivialise the despair that good men and women must face, as God remains in cloud and darkness.

But is there anything positive to be said on the matter? Is the elusiveness of God at times simply part of what we have to accept, God's business and not ours? Is it something the purpose of which we may see in the life to come when we are no longer seeing puzzling reflections in a mirror? A generation ago, the term for this approach was 'eschatological verification', meaning simply that when our life was over we would be in a position to verify the truth of our religious propositions ...

But, in the later middle ages, some of the great writers on
spirituality explored the idea that this hidden-ness of God was
in fact an essential experience on the road of spiritual matur-
ing. St John of the Cross wrote that God intentionally leads the
soul on a path of dark contemplation and spiritual dryness
where it seems to be lost.[11] And St John gives his reasons. The
genuine seeker for God, he believes, must strip himself or
herself of desire for worldly success or possessions. That
search cannot come about in brightness. In other words,
Robert Browning's Victorian assertion that 'God's in his
heaven, All's right with the world' is in fact a deceitful image.
When the world is at its glamorous brightest, God usually
ceases to matter

The road which the disciple takes is a road of faith, and this
road is cloud and darkness to the intellect in isolation. There
is a nuance here that is important, because it runs to the very
edge of a very dangerous doctrine, the idea that faith is
irrational. St John is not saying that. He is arguing that the
road of faith will diverge from intellect alone, and that
intellect alone will flounder in the processes of faith. God is
the goal and end of our religious quest, and he is beyond
human sight. He is ultimate light, and this total light appears
as darkness to purely human brightness. We might wish to give
this image of light and darkness a different pivot, and say that
if God is ultimate meaning, then our human anthropomorphic notions of meaning will seem futile and confusing in
contrast. We find ourselves in the disorientation and vulnerability characteristic of any no-man's land where escape seems
the only desirable action.

The real problem, as St John sees it, is that very often it is
not God we are seeking, but other things, such as inner peace

11. On this, and on the discussion below, St John of the Cross's *The Ascent of
Mount Carmel* and *The Dark Night of the Soul, passim*. See also Kenneth
Leech, *True God*, 1985, London, Sheldon Press, SPCK, chapter 6.

or spiritual harmony or what might loosely be described as
'spirituality'. But they are not on offer. If one wishes to see
God, everything else must be abandoned, even the fruits of
spirituality we most seek. We cannot even demand understanding or meaning or personal 'being'.

There is a moving moment in Camus' semi-autobiographi-
cal novel *The First Man* where, as a forty year-old, 'Jacques'
stands for the first time in front of the grave of his father who
had been killed in the First World War at the age of twenty-
nine. Not only does Jacques have to come to terms with the
fact that his father is now almost his child, given that he is now
so much older than was his father when he died, but also that
there is an almost eternal frustration in the meaninglessness
of it all.

> All that was left was this anguished heart, eager to live,
> rebelling against the deadly order of the world that had
> been with him for forty years, and still struggling against
> the wall that separated him from the secret of all life,
> wanting to go further, to go beyond, and to discover,
> discover before dying, discover at last in order to be, just
> for a single second, but for ever.[12]

But not even that is on offer. In seeking God, we can seek
nothing else, not even what it means to be in existence, even
for a single second.

There is, in the writings of St John of the Cross, the
straightforward enough suggestion that the contrast between
God's greatness and our faltering understanding of him is so
great that we will inevitably find that this chasm brings us to
the point of dislocation. In other words, God's brightness and
our notions of brightness simply do not belong to the same
realm of being. The twentieth century theologian Paul Tillich

---

12. Albert Camus, *TheFirstMan*, trans. David Hapgood, 1995, Harmondsworth,
    Penguin Books, p. 21.

made something of the same point when he spoke about the feeling we all have at times of wanting to escape from this uncomfortable God. As he would remind us, the person who has never tried to escape God has never experienced a real God. There is no reason to flee a God who is only the perfect picture of everything that is good in us, or who is simply the universe, or who 'is' the laws of nature, or the course of history. There is no point in trying to escape a God who is nothing more than a kind father who guarantees our immortality and eternal bliss. Why should we try to escape from someone who is so useful to us? No, suggests Tillich, this is not the vision of God , but rather of a human trying to make God in his own image and for his own comfort. In other words, if it is the real God (and not simply the God of our creation, made in our image), then he cannot neatly conform to human categorisation.

*The Cloud of Unknowing* (of unknown authorship) is one of the great classics of the English spiritual tradition of the fourteenth century. This was a tradition, remarkably vigorous, rugged, often earthy and humorous in its effect, but also of extraordinary spiritual insight, which included Dame Julian of Norwich, Walter Hilton and Margery Kempe. *The Cloud of Unknowing* is of importance in its insistence that the only way of penetrating the cloud that comes between us and God is what the writer describes as the intention to love, and to love only God. Leaving behind what he or she calls a cloud of forgetting (by which is meant the compulsions, illusions and manipulations of the world's priorities), the remaining cloud, this cloud of unknowing, still stands between us and God. But God's love for us can give us the will to penetrate the cloud with our own love for God – 'a sharp dart of longing love', to use the writer's own phrase. What we, who are probably not contemplatives, may surely grasp from St John of the Cross or *The Cloud of Unknowing* is that if we can somehow hang on to love or real altruism, and let go of the possible benefits (even the spiritual benefits) of an encounter with God, then the shadows may become slightly penetrable. The vulnerability is still there, a no-man's land is still there – but so, we can trust, is God.

Wilfred Owen was remembered, by those with whom he served, for his genuine love and care for those under his command. Perhaps this is why for him, God could be seen, not so much through a cloud, as through mud.

# 3

# The Accidental Watch

From what we see around us, is there any good reason to believe in God? The arguments for the existence of God which pursue this line of inquiry, in other words begin with the world as we perceive it, and work from there to an adduced necessity for a Creator (the so-called cosmological arguments), are many and are remarkably varied, in both complexity and subtlety.

Probably the most readily accessible of these is a famous argument of an eighteenth century English archdeacon, William Paley. His 'argument from design' is not so much an argument as a parable. In essence, he suggests that if, while out walking, we were by chance to come upon a watch lying on the ground, it would never occur to us to think that the watch, with its complicated mechanism and obvious function and design, could be some sort of chance happening. In other words, it must have been made, and have had a mind behind its making. Paley goes on to suggest that any objective consideration of the world in which humanity is set would come to the same conclusion. The world, he suggests, is clearly too complex, too laden with purpose and function, to have just 'happened'. There is therefore a Mind and a Creator behind the world, *QED*

Although enticing and encouraging, Paley's argument from design cannot hold up on strictly logical grounds. In the first place, we cannot logically take an objective view of a structure of which we ourselves are an integral part, for we have nothing with which to compare it. We are inside the 'machine', if it is one, and we cannot look at it in the detached way that we can look at a watch on the ground. Ludwig Wittgenstein put the matter very straightforwardly in the

*Tractatus Logico-Philosophicus* when he said that

> the sense of the world must lie outside the world. For all
> happening and being-so is accidental. What makes it
> non-accidental cannot lie in the world, for otherwise this
> would again be accidental. It must lie outside the world.
> (6.41)

In addition, the amount we know today of the sheer scale
of the universe also weakens Paley's central point considerably. At the turn of the third millennium, we might well feel
inclined to say that, for all we know, this world is a particularly
bad, crude and clumsy mechanism in comparison to other
planets, millions of light years away, the existence of which is
now known to us, but which we have never experienced. The
chances of a complex world such as ours having developed,
complete with beings capable of thinking and philosophising
about life and death might seem slim, but if there are trillions
upon trillions upon trillions of such planets in the totality of
known and unknown space, then, sooner or later, something
strange of this kind just happening might not seem a statistical
nonsense. The cosmological arguers may (and do) counter
this with the initial question 'But who started the whole thing
going?'

Given how little we continue to know about the beginnings
of the universe, this question sounds suspiciously like the
application of a process of reasoning derived from the human
experience of cause and effect to realms in which that experience may or may not apply. There does however, remain an
enticing question, posed (however tentatively and briefly) by
Stephen Hawking in *A Brief History of Time,* when he points out
that even if there is only one possible unified theory, it is just
a set of rules and equations. But, he goes on to ask,

> ... what is it that breathes fire into the equations and
> makes a universe for them to describe? The usual ap-

proach of science of constructing a mathematical model
cannot answer the question of why there should be a
universe for the model to describe. Why does the universe go to all the bother of existing? Is the unified
theory so compelling that it brings about its own existence? Or does it need a creator and, if so, does he have
any other effect on the universe? [1]

There are those who would say, with some passion, that the
supposed 'design' of nature is not suggestive of a good, loving,
and compassionate God, and who use this as the explosive for
the demolition of religious belief.

Perhaps the most passionate of the present generation of
scientific atheists is Richard Dawkins. Following the Darwinian thread of reasoning, he would point us (in one now fairly
well-known example) to the species of 'digger wasps'. [2] A
female digger wasp not only lays her egg within a caterpillar,
so that the larvae may feed on its flesh, but she carefully uses
her sting to paralyse the caterpillar so that it can do nothing
about the fact that it is being eaten alive, and slowly at that.
From a human perspective we would think of this as torture,
give it a moral context, and wonder why a loving Creator
might not have found a less cruel way to order the needs of
nature. Dawkins argues that it is ridiculous to think of the
activities of a digger wasp inside the body of a caterpillar as
'cruel'.

A better notion would be that of utter indifference. Only
when we are obsessed with the questions of 'Why?' does any
notion of nature's cruelty intrude. Dawkins would argue that
there is no reason to ask the question 'Why?' of such occurrences, and he then extrapolates his argument compellingly.
We have equally, he would suggest, no reason to ask the

1.  Stephen Hawking, *A Brief History of Time*, 1996, Bantam Press, p. 209.
2.  Richard Dawkins, *River out of Eden*, 1995, London, Weidenfeld and Nichol-
    son, p. 95 ff.

question 'Why?' when a child is ravaged by cancer or when an earthquake wreaks its horror. Because science is largely concerned with the question 'How?' does not mean, Dawkins suggests, that there is necessarily another and ancillary question 'Why?', waiting in the wings to be asked. In short, the fact that one may logically frame the question 'Why?' does not mean that it is a legitimate question to ask. Evolution has produced humans as nothing more than survival machines; genetically we are coded to ensure the continuing survival of our ilk.

It clearly causes Dawkins great aggravation that there should be people around who feel that they are in a position to ask the question 'Why?' But this is nothing to the aggravation caused for him by those who wish to suggest that there might be an answer to the question. Dawkin's fairly rigid evolutionary stance has of course not gone unchallenged by other scientists. And, although a dispute between scientists is a territory where the non-scientist should maintain a dignified silence, it should surely be noted that there are scientists (of whom the Harvard palaeontologist Stephen Jay Gould seems at present to be the most vociferous), who would say that there is a necessary 'randomness' within the unfolding of creation.

When Einstein said in a famous epigram that God does not play dice, he was talking science rather than theology. There are, however, certain parallel arguments within science which predicate that only with a built-in randomness, the metaphorical throwing of a dice whether by God or an abstract creation, can we 'make sense' of how human intelligence develops within both the species as a whole and within individuals. Even if an apparent randomness within the creative process could be definitively established it would not of course thereby prove God's existence. But Dawkins would not even opt for the term 'randomness'. He is a great deal more subtle than he is sometimes given credit for. In his book *The Blind Watchmaker*, he makes an important distinction between randomness and natural selection.[3] He is full of enthusiasm, even of awe, for the beauty and intricacy of the workings of nature and the inter-relationship and inter-dependence between the different aspects of nature. He is certain that the explanation is to be found in an inherent determination to survive, within genes themselves. That is their only purpose. They did not need an external creator to give them such a purpose.

The tenor and thrust of the debate underlines the fact that a scientific atheist such as Dawkins is in fact a philosopher. To say, in effect, that for all that there is much in the world that is awesome and wonderful, there are still no grounds for believing that it could all have been designed by a Creator (or at any rate by a good Creator) is more or less a moral judgement. And to say that it is of no purpose to ask the question 'Why?' is most certainly a profoundly philosophical proposition.

This is all said, not to suggest that Dawkins' arguments lack force, for he certainly points to major practical shortcomings in any bland argument from design. One might, however, wish to suggest that we should not fall into the trap of mistaking atheism as the necessary and only stance for a scientist. Without over-simplifying the matter, the searching for a reason , the asking of the question 'Why?', is something that people do in everyday life all the time, and over the most mundane of issues – 'Why did he say that?' or 'Why doesn't she do this?' Is there any axiomatic reason why the question 'Why?' cannot logically be directed at more major questions, such as whether there is or is not a connection between a particular individual occurrence and an underlying context of purpose or meaning? If one might have a genuine hope for

3.  Richard Dawkins, *The Blind Watchmaker*, 1996, W. W. Norton and Co., chapters 1 and 2.

the future of the relationship between religious belief and science, it would be that both the God-talker and the science-talker would begin to accept the degree of provisionality in what both are saying. This would mean that both would accept that their thoughts may well impinge on the other's thoughts, but that when they contradict one another it is because either the scientist is talking God-talk (or non-God talk), or because the theologian has decided that he is a scientist. It might also of course be because one of them is simply talking nonsense, under either heading.

Having said that there may be an area of stimulating dialogue, it should be added that the explication of theology from a purely scientific perspective may only be embarked upon properly by scientists. Without intruding into it, it does seem that at least two important lines of argument within this general area may usefully be developed by those who are, scientifically, laymen.

The first is that, whatever about the apparent weaknesses in the design of the world in which we live, it is apparently becoming more complex all the time, and more complex than is necessary to fit with a strict Darwinian view which sees survival as the fundamental dynamic. Intellectual capacity has done far more than simply to enable humanity to survive. To put it another way, if a human is indeed only a survival machine, he or she has done far more than he need have done. It does not necessarily follow that humankind could have conceived of immortality only if that were a possibility, but there must be the eerie impression that humanity has developed too far, and continues to develop intellectual capacity too much (albeit sometimes with hideous results), if the only thing we can say about humankind is that it wishes to survive and that it cannot bear too much reality.

If humankind has gone unnecessarily far in the development of intellectual capacity, this is even more pronounced when we turn to artistic achievement, which has very little to do with a survival machine. The fact that (as John Polkinghorne puts it) we rebel at the thought that the sun's explosion and the eventual collapse or decay of the whole universe will render futile Shakespeare and Mozart and St Francis and their achievements is not, in itself, evidence of anything (for it may still be mere wishful thinking that the sun will not explode). But it does surely suggest that a strictly mechanical view of the universe may not be the only solution to questions of existence.[4]

The second strand, developed by the philosopher Richard Swinburne, concerns an important distinction between credulity and scepticism. The rational man, argues Swinburne, is the credulous man, who trusts experience until it is found to lead him astray, whereas the sceptic is the person who refuses to trust experience until it is been established that it is not misleading him.[5] The demands of scientific enquiry will inevitably lean towards the latter. But that is not the only aspect of truth. There is something to be said for trusting experience, one's own and that of others, until it is clearly shown to be flawed. We do not thereby believe absolutely anything until it is positively disproved. The question of extra-terrestrials arriving on earth to abduct humans is one which has never been disproved, but it is surely one on which many people would remain sceptical until some satisfactory proof is established. On such a matter we are prepared to remain, in the proper sense of the word, *agnostic*.

Here again, if we return to the imagery of no-man's land, there is surely a place for reason and truth within a no-man's land where neither the entirely credulous nor the entirely sceptical are safe. Religious belief may find its own reality in precisely such a place, between an unconditional credulity

---

4. John Polkinghorne, *Science and Christian Belief*, 1994, London, SPCK, p. 18.
5. R. G. Swinburne, *The Existence of God*, 1979. Oxford, Oxford University Press, p 13.

and an unconditional scepticism.

None of this defeats the arguments which would reject belief in God, or at any rate belief in a god who is more than a cosmic watchmaker who sets the universe in motion and simply looks on, as it proceeds in its own way. If we believe that there are grounds for believing in God, are we bound to believe only in one who winds up his toy and lets it operate for as long as it can without intervention of any kind (in other words, the God of what is traditionally called Deism)? Or, alternatively, must we believe in a God who will constantly interrupt the world of nature and who will at times intervene in the world, even in the most trivial of ways? Or, as a third possibility, must we seek a place between those trenches?

If we are inclined to believe in a God who has not relinquished all control and even all interest in his creation, the principal conundrum we face is the age-old one as to why the design seems so manifestly unfair and unjust. In other words, why is there a cruelty in nature, a cruelty which Dawkins sees only as indifference? The question will never be solved, and for many, it has been the principal reason for the unworkability of faith. For others, it is only the existence of a world which is not entirely 'fair' in its distribution of good and ill that will permit humanity to operate with moral freedom. If there is a God who is more than a theory to breathe fire into the equations and rules of existence, and who has a genuine interest in events on earth, and who, more particularly, had a purpose in creating the world (other than as a bizarre and rather disgusting experiment), then that purpose can only be the personal and free 'growth' of the created. Growth of the whole person is possible only when there is a growth in moral functioning.

Can one be a moral creature when the immediate results of good behaviour are instant rewards and the immediate results of bad behaviour are instant punishments? The answer must surely be 'No'. At the heart of truly moral behaviour is the thought that one may choose a path that was not moral and yet remain unpunished. If an individual's good health were the direct result of a predilection for helping old people across busy roads, old people would not only be persecuted with attempts to drag them across roads they did not wish to cross, but the motivation for such apparent 'kindness' would not be moral goodness but simple prudence. Similarly, if an attempt to swindle one's neighbour automatically resulted in a heavy dose of 'flu, neighbours might not be swindled, but the reason would have nothing to do with moral behaviour, only with common sense. There must be a degree of uncertainty and even randomness, objectively speaking, in nature's dealing with individual people, if morality or any form of unselfishness is to be an option.

There is of course an underlying assumption here that unselfishness and moral reasoning are indications of 'value' in an individual human. We might certainly suggest, as some semblance of evidence, that altruism, along with gratitude, is very often the last 'skill' to be attained in a child, and is the first to be jettisoned in old age. Whether that makes it a higher virtue may, of course, be questioned. Altruistic moral goodness is, however, something which can only exist where there is not a simple system of instant rewards and punishments in operation. There can only be moral goodness in a world where nature does not function on a strictly moral basis. That is relatively easy to say (or write) as an intellectual solution to an abstract conundrum. It is probably of no help whatsoever to those who have to care for a cancer-eaten child or an Altzheimers-diseased parent for every moment of every day.

In his novel *The Plague*, Camus gives sharp expression to the intractable problem of evil and suffering. A terrible plague grips the town of Oran, killing scores of victims every day. The doctor Rieux, an unbeliever, finds the attitude of the priest,

Paneloux, very difficult to accept. In an early stage in the book, Paneloux preaches about the plague as a form of divine judgement on the town.

Rieux's friend Tarrou asks him at one point whether he believes in God. The doctor replies:

> 'No – but what does that really mean? I'm fumbling in the dark, struggling to make something out. But I've long ceased finding that original....'
>
> 'Isn't that it – the gulf between Paneloux and you?'
>
> 'I doubt it. Paneloux is a man of learning, a scholar. He hasn't come in contact with death; that's why he can speak with such assurance of the truth – with a capital T. But every country priest who visits his parishioners, and has heard a man gasping for breath on his deathbed, thinks as I do. He'd try to relieve human suffering before trying to point out its excellence.' Rieux stood up: his face was now in shadow. 'Let's drop the subject,' he said, 'as you won't answer.'
>
> Tarrou remained seated in his chair; he was smiling again. 'Suppose I answer with a question?'
>
> The doctor now smiled, too.
>
> 'You like being mysterious, don't you? ... Yes, fire away.'
>
> 'My question's this,' said Tarrou. 'Why do you yourself show such devotion, considering you don't believe in God? I suspect your answer may help me to mine.'
>
> His face still in shadow, Rieux said that he'd already answered: that if he believed in an all-powerful God he would cease curing the sick and leave that to Him. But no one in the world believed in a God of that sort; no, not even Paneloux, who believed that he believed in such a God.[6]

---

6. Albert Camus, *The Plague*, trans. Stuart Gilbert, 1960. Harmondsworth, Penguin Books, p. 107.

There is a point further on in the book, when Rieux and Paneloux have together been with a child who has just died. Rieux gives vent to his feelings and turns on Paneloux, telling him that that child was innocent of anything wrong. He then strides out of the building.

He heard a voice behind him.

'Why was there that anger in your voice just now? What we'd been seeing was as unbearable to me as it was to you.' Rieux turned towards Paneloux.

'1 know. I'm sorry. But weariness is a kind of madness. And there are times when the only feeling I have is one of mad revolt.'

'I understand,' Paneloux said in a low voice. 'That sort of thing is revolting because it passes our human understanding. But perhaps we should love what we cannot understand.'

Rieux straightened up slowly. He gazed at Paneloux, summoning to his gaze all the strength and fervour he could muster against his weariness. Then he shook his head.

'No, Father. I've a very different idea of love. And until my dying day I shall refuse to love a scheme of things in which children are put to torture.'

A shade of disquietude crossed the priest's face. He was silent for a moment. Then, 'Ah, doctor,' he said sadly, 'I've just realised what is meant by "grace".'

Rieux had sunk back again on the bench. His lassitude had returned and from its depths he spoke, more gently.

'It's something I haven't got; that I know. But I'd rather not discuss that with you. We're working side by side for something that unites us – beyond blasphemy and prayers. And it's the only thing that matters.' [7]

7.  Camus, *The Plague*, p. 178.

There can be no smart intellectual answer to the questions of suffering, innocent suffering in particular. But it must nevertheless be said that in the centre of any moral argument for or against the existence of a good God, there seems to be a place for a new understanding of the Incarnation which would see Christ himself as being in a moral no-man's land on the cross, as both ultimately responsible (being God), and also as the unavenged victim of freewill (being crucified).

This does present a coherence which is compelling. And it is precisely why the point in the narrative of the crucifixion, where Christ rebels against the unfairness of it all is a pivotal point in the entire Gospel. The words, 'My God, my God, why have you forsaken me?' carry all the dread and vulnerability of no-man's land. Christ is, in orthodox Christian thinking, the fullness of deity. As such, he is in control of everything, and must therefore bear ultimate responsibility. Christ on the cross is also, within Christian orthodoxy, the fullness of a helpless and defenceless human frailty, destroyed by the callousness and cruelty of humans at their worst – the victim. There is a position here that is full of internal contradiction and conflict, in every sense a no-man's land, with entrenched humanity on the one side and entrenched deity on the other. And the words, 'My God, my God, why have you forsaken me?' thus carry a strange and extraordinary strength. It is therefore scarcely surprising that it is to this outburst of Christ (and sometimes only to those words) that at least some of the suffering, the tortured, the dying of humanity through the ages have been able to cling, for hope of some coherence in connecting to eternity.

This is all a far remove from Archdeacon Paley's walk, and it is most certainly not a proof of God's existence. What it may suggest, however, is that a doctrine of the Incarnation, how-ever mediated and interpreted, however distorted in the course of mediation, has at least an integrity which can speak

to a world where the freedom of nature is for the most part left
to its own devises. It is a world which is a very far remove from
a Garden of Eden, but it may well be the only place to which
cosmological arguments for God's existence will lead us.

The metaphor of Garden of Eden is of a place of ultimate
certainties, but also (of its very nature), without emotion or
freedom, for good or ill. Eden was a certain place – without
problems, without struggles. We might also wish to ask if it was
not also probably rather boring. The Garden of Eden would
have been tidy, orderly, and in strict accordance with a
properly designed cosmos that might even have impressed a
Dawkins. And yet so much of what it is to be truly human can
only be found outside such a place. Edwin Muir in his
remarkable poem *One Foot in Eden* expressed it evocatively:

> But famished field and blackened tree
> Bear flowers in Eden never known.
> Blossoms of grief and charity
> Bloom in those darkened fields alone.
> What had Eden ever to say
> Of hope and faith and pity and love
> Until was buried all its day
> And memory found its treasure trove?
> Strange blessings never in Paradise
> Fall from these beclouded skies.[8]

Whether the possibility of the charity makes up for the
certainty of the grief, and begins to make the entire edifice
worth it, would be hotly disputed by Dr Rieux. But it is surely
the only thing that may give a coherence to something that
may be far more than a watch on a large scale, or even more
than a giant coincidence.

---

8.   Edwin Muir, *Collected Poems*, 1963. London, Faber and Faber.

# 4

# Between Saturn and Mercury

One of the issues that will emerge immediately upon acceptance of any belief that individual humans do and should connect with something objective beyond them is that there may be a responsibility to that which is beyond. A secondary issue is the question as to whether that which is beyond, the external or the extrinsic, can be a guide for behaviour or belief.

In the twelfth of his *Last Poems*,[1] A. E. Housman is engaged in a search for objective guidance or direction; it is almost certain that he wrestled at the time with the reality of his own homosexuality.

> The laws of God, the laws of men,
> He may keep, that will and can;
> Not I: let God and man decree
> Laws for themselves and not for me;
> And if my ways are not as theirs
> Let them mind their own affairs.
> Their deeds I judge and much condemn,
> Yet when did I make laws for them?
> Please yourselves, say I, and they
> Need only look the other way.
> But no, they will not; they must still
> Wrest their neighbour to their will,
> And make me dance as they desire
> With jail and gallows and hell-fire.
> And how am I to face the odds
> Of man's bedevilment and God's?
> I, a stranger and afraid

1. *The Works of A.E. Housman*, 1994. London, Wordsworth Editions.

In a world I never made.
They will be master, right or wrong;
Though both are foolish, both are strong.
And since, my soul, we cannot fly
To Saturn nor to Mercury,
Keep we must, if keep we can,
These foreign laws of God and man.

This is a passionate cry far distant from any unthinking acceptance of the authority of the external. Here is a demand for individualism and for individual freedom in a frightening and inexplicable world. Yet there is an allusion at the end of the poem which shows just why such a stance of individuality is logically and philosophically impossible –

Since, my soul, we cannot fly
To Saturn nor to Mercury.

Saturn is usually identified with Kronos, the Greek god who was ruler of the world in the age of innocence. Mercury, as well as being a messenger for the gods , was also the Roman god of thieves. Housman therefore sees the impossibility of moving either to Saturn – that is, beyond the need for an objective moral framework – or to Mercury – that is, beyond a need for the enforcement of objective moral values. They are two freedoms, we might say, at the opposite ends of the spectrum, and both are totally beyond human reach. Hence,

Keep we must, if keep we can,
These foreign laws of God and man.

What should now be done is to tease out the inherent contradictions, as we reach the two ends of the spectrum, the extremes that I would now want to describe as total heteronomy and total autonomy, using 'heteronomy' to mean that which is governed only by external laws and principles, and 'autonomy' to mean that which is decided by one's own laws and principles.

Heteronomy may denote the law of the land, or the principles of the Bible, or the commands of a Church or sect. It would be interesting to trace the history of people who have tried to merge all three sources of heteronomous authority – in other words a strict adherence to biblical, ecclesiastical and political demands – as part of a pure obedience to a single and integrated authority. Calvin certainly attempted it in Geneva, as did the Pilgrim Fathers in New England and the Mormons in Utah. Sooner or later, however, the world turns out to be too small and inter-related for the different forms of heteronomous authority not to fall out with one another. In practice, most groups will usually attempt only two out of three modes of obedience to the outside authority. Fundamentalist sects, for example, would often claim to combine the 'ecclesiastical' and biblical, albeit without using the term 'ecclesiastical'. In other cases, Churches in totalitarian states (as in Nazi Germany) have tried to merge ecclesiastical with political calls for obedience. And powerful Churches, as we know, have tried to bend governments to their own ecclesiastical fundamentals (but rarely, it has to be said, to truly biblical fundamentals).

Returning to the inherent flaws in a total heteronomy, it has to be recognised that, in practice, supposedly objective 'principles' are always being filtered, processed and revised by individuals. This may take various forms.

Sometimes it will come through a group or community leader's particular mode of revisionism. The leader's unchallenged autonomy allows him or her to hack away at a supposedly objective heteronomy all the time. So there may well be a total divergence between individual biblical fundamentalist leaders on what a passage of Scripture means, even though each will be convinced that they are submitting to the heteronomous authority of Scripture. The only thing that they may have in common is that each one just knows that he or she (usually 'he') is right.

There is, equally, a constant 'revision' of political fundamentals by its leadership. Marxism, from the moment Marx
finished writing, was being altered, and sometimes radically,
although none of those who were basically re-writing Marx
(whether Lenin, Trotsky, Stalin or Mao) would have admitted
that they were doing anything other than correctly interpret-
ing the true Marx, the true heteronomous fundamentals for
Communism. And the different mainline Christian Churches
are equally expert in interpolating useful alterations into
their supposedly heteronomous God-given tradition.

But, secondly, if supposedly heteronomous fundamentals
are constantly processed by the individual leaders of the
group or community, they are also being filtered consciously
and unconsciously by the individual adherents. The followers
either don't quite 'hear' the whole message or, more particularly, they don't quite 'hear' the inconvenient bits. This is easy
to mock. We may readily criticise those who claim to be 'Bible
Christians' but who have not noticed the incredibly tough Old
Testament demands of financial generosity to the outsider
who cannot possibly repay a debt. There may also be the loyal
member of the party in government who doesn't believe that
income tax provisions introduced by the party and enacted
for the country as a whole actually apply to him or her. In some
cases, this may be hypocrisy. But very often it is but a selective
use of the heteronomous, and this will always be the actuality,
for autonomy will inevitably hack away at heteronomy.

Two further brief points on a heteronomy at its extremes
should be noted. The first is a tendency to splinter among the
more authoritarian manifestations of supposed heteronomy,
because the requirements of individualism will always in-
fringe. Either the group leadership expels those who are
showing dissent (and may well imprison or execute them if it
is given the opportunity), or a splinter group voluntarily sets

up independently with revised fundamentals which, needless to say, this new group will argue are the true heteronomous principles. This accounts for the proliferation of religious sects, just as it explains the capacity of Irish republicanism – and unionism too – to fragment into new and ever purer off-shoots. Sometimes the original group, if it is powerful enough, will hang on grimly to the dissidents and force them into line, with either physical or spiritual pressure. As Housman puts it,

> … they must still
> Wrest their neighbour to their will,
> And make me dance as they desire
> With jail and gallows and hell-fire.

There is a further area in this context into which it would be unwise to delve too deeply as it is undoubtedly intruding into an area of clinical psychology where only experts should roam. Having made that admission, it may surely be suggested (almost as an axiom) that the person who is genuinely and totally a fundamentalist – a 'victim' of ultimate heteronomy, whether political, ecclesiastical, or biblical – who is therefore not using any powers of personal analysis or discrimination, is quite clearly in a pathological condition. He or she has either been manipulated or brain-washed out of any autonomy (as some people undoubtedly have been), or else, by some flaw of nature, they never had any proper autonomy, or an illness or injury removed it from them.

A thoroughgoing mechanistic perspective on the universe would argue that this is just wishful thinking, and would suggest further that no-one is truly autonomous at all. We are only what external causes have made us. Our thoughts, our actions, our sense of having control, are not ours. They have all been created by factors external to ourselves. There is a rather obvious logical contradiction here: for if all our thoughts are conditioned by external factors, then even that thought – that we have no autonomy – is itself the consequence of external factors, and cannot have any greater intrinsic validity than the external factors which make a man think that he is autonomous, or even that he is a banana.

If we were to move to the other end of the spectrum, where is the problem with a personal philosophy which is entirely autonomous, where one is only governed by one's own laws and principles? The answer is that, logically, it too becomes self-contradictory, as soon as one tries to move beyond self. The only completely autonomous thought we may have is that we may possibly exist. Even our own existence only has meaning in relation to the existence of other people..

But, if we leave philosophy to one side, to live in community means that we respond to, and accept, the demands and restrictions that the existence of others imposes on us. In the real world, we cannot sustain the viewpoint that every one can make up his or her own philosophy and then act upon it, regardless of community. Reckoning in a purely autonomous manner, Hitler was not only entitled to his personal views but (because they had as much validity as any one else's) he also had the same inalienable rights to base his life and activities on his philosophy, even if that were to mean murdering millions of Jews and hence depriving them of their equal right to autonomy. We cannot have complete autonomy in community, as even Housman concedes – 'Keep we must if keep we can, / These foreign laws of God and man', for which we might substitute 'these *heteronomous* laws of God and man'.

The truth seems therefore to be that we cannot be completely autonomous; neither can we be completely at the disposal of heteronomous forces. We cannot be completely individualistic and we cannot be completely at the disposal of community. We have to live and work somewhere on the spectrum between the two extremes, in that no-man's land.

And if we are therefore no longer entitled to say, 'Because I say that, it is therefore right' (autonomy) or to say 'Because he or she or it says that, it is therefore right' (heteronomy), are we thereby compelled to flounder around in a total relativism, and to say that nothing is ever objectively right and nothing is objectively wrong? Or must we say further that nothing other than an empirically verifiable fact or a mathematical proposition is ultimately 'true' or 'untrue'? Rather than lingering in the sterility of the extremities of autonomy and heteronomy, it is, surely, of more value to consider the creative aspects of living in a tension between the two. This is, after all, something immensely constructive, because it is what makes us human, rather than puppets on another's string, whether God's, man's or woman's.

I mentioned the Garden of Eden in the context of Edwin Muir's poem, *One Foot in Eden*, and the fact that Eden had little to say to love, to emotion, to grief. Because it has all the answers, what does any absolutist code have to communicate, in Muir's terms, of faith and hope and pity and love? Does it have, or can it have 'blossoms of grief and charity'? But those 'strange blessings' are certainly to be found on that uneasy no-man's land that wends its way between the trenches of total individualism and an imposed fundamentalism.

If we can accept the positive aspects of moving beyond the imposed certainties of fundamentalism, does that still mean that we have no choice but to take on a philosophy of relativism? There is an evocative phrase in the thirty-first Psalm which reads (in the Anglican Book of Common Prayer version), 'Thou hast set my feet in a large room ... ' Without overloading the metaphor, it is worth noting that it is a large room, not a dungeon, because we have a degree of autonomy. And, although large, it is a room, and therefore it has walls and limitations, because there must be a degree of heteronomy also. As we seek God or truth, love, holiness or salvation, or just happiness, we must identify some boundaries, as otherwise our pursuit is so autonomous as to be aimless. But we have also to be wary, in most settings, about designing large rooms for others, although I think that we may suggest logical limits for some contexts of exploration.

We see this most obviously as individuals within society. We have to have defined walls, however open a society we might wish to produce. These walls are surely those of damage-limitation. We must limit the damage that individuals may do to others either by commission or omission. We may wish to say that the limits will include protection of all from physical violence, will include equality of opportunity, and will include political accountability. We might all devise our own ideal states, but that is not really the purpose of this discussion. What is, however, germane to the matter is that if we are to jettison political fundamentalism, we accept that there is a fair amount of 'baggage' that goes out with it. One thing, for example, which cannot be essential to the regulation of an open society is the mythology behind nationalism or community loyalty of any kind. If we were to allow a place for cherished national myth in our political philosophy we are slipping down into a dangerous heteronomy, which gives 'nationalism' or 'tradition' a spurious intrinsic validity.

When we turn to the faith, or to the Church, what may we provide that is not restrictive and absolutist, and yet which has some boundaries? Because any blueprint is by its nature heteronomous, we might have use for a set of markers when we ask the question 'Where do we place frontiers on the Christian Church?' And we cannot say that there need be none. We could not, for example, reasonably contain genuine black magic within the Christian Church, if the word 'Christian' were to retain any meaning. By way of example and moving into highly personal mode, I am not certain that, as a believing Christian, I need place the walls around the specifically Christian faith closer together than the affirmation that Christ is a unique and decisive disclosure of God in humanity,

and that his earthly life not only shows us uniquely the reality
of God, but does in a mysterious way effect a reconciliation
between God and believing men and women. Likewise I
would not wish, from a Christian viewpoint, to place the walls
around the status of the Bible closer together than the
affirmation that the Bible is of unique significance in its value
as revealing and disclosing to us a God who has an objective
reality. For some people, this would all be risibly restrictive.
For others, it would be fuzzy liberalism of the worst kind. But
that is because it is between two trenches. In more positive
mode, it would seem obvious that any understanding of
Christ, from any Christian perspective, will point to the
primacy of love in relationships.

It is a role of the Church to explore and underline the
implications of that central teaching, but without threaten-
ing. So there are walls, and there will even be such a thing as
sin. But the walls that are there should be for purposes of
demarcation, but never function as walls of defence or of
hostility. In other words, what the Church may not do is, in
Housman's language, 'to wrest their neighbour to their will'.
The neighbour who chooses to remain outside the walls is
entitled to be there. It is the state's business, but not the
Church's business, to stop him or her damaging those around.
Christ was crucified outside the walls, but he did not crucify
others outside the walls.

# 5

# Somewhere over the Rainbow

The idea of a life beyond the conclusion of a human life on this earth is one which, for most adherents of Christianity, is a *sine qua non* for signing up to the rest of the Christian package. For many, although by no means all, there seems little point to the rest of the agenda of love and redemption, if life on earth is all there is to personal existence. But not for all. The Cambridge theologian Don Cupitt passionately implores his readers that, if they are truly to understand Christian redemption, they must first discard what he calls a 'barmy fantasy' of life after death.[1] He sees this dream of life beyond death as a sad wish-fulfilment that must be abandoned if the true message of Christianity is to be grasped. This message is that in order to conquer death we must, before we die, die to death and to self. This, for Cupitt, is true redemption. Everything else is self-deception and mirage.

It is certainly true that we cannot reasonably claim that life after death is somehow 'built in' to the apparatus of creation. And what little we might learn from the explorations and experiences of spiritualism is so thoroughly ambiguous and deeply personal as to add nothing by way of proof to the possibility of life beyond the grave. From the explorations of spiritualists we might reasonably suggest the likelihood of a great deal more psychic communication than science has as yet explained, but we would be unwarranted in taking the argument a great deal further, largely because the information which is assumed to come from beyond the grave may as easily have arrived subliminally, unconsciously (and without any charlatan intent) from some other person still living.

---

1. Don Cupitt, *The New Christian Ethics* , 1988, London, SCM Press, p. 67.

After all, 'information received' by means of spiritualism may only be verified as true or coherent if some other person, still living, can verify it. The question remains, therefore, as to whether, without recourse to spiritualism or a strictly literalist use of Scripture, we may consider an after-life as reasonable, and possibly true.

It seems logical to suggest that if the existence of love is genuinely the key for predicating both meaning to life on earth, and the probability that life is under God, then we may argue for an existence beyond this one on earth. This does not make life after death an integral or natural part of the way that life on earth runs; it is rather the logical consequence of finding some 'loving' resolution to the tangled threads and unfilled sectors of an earthly life. This type of reasoning runs along these lines: if we are loved by God, then our non-existence at any stage in the future cannot be his will. This is admittedly blatant anthropomorphism, as an extrapolation from the certainty that a human who loved another would never wish for the other's non-existence. But it is an established argument, used by William Temple among others, and it is still worth consideration. What it is suggesting is that whereas it is wrong to think of an after-life as a right or as somehow natural, this does not thereby make it unreasonable. If there is any purpose behind creation, that purpose is manifestly not resolved within the limits of life on earth. The only mode of resolution is a life beyond this one where everything, to put it crudely, is straightened out. In other words, if the resolution of the purpose of creation is not in this life, it must be somewhere else.

It has to be admitted immediately that this does not seem either attractive or necessary for everyone. The French writer Simone de Beauvoir put the matter bluntly when she remarked that she would have detested it if the part that was being played out here below already had its *dénouement* in eternity, but that is perhaps not precisely the same thing in that it presupposes a cosmic determinism.

We have to add that the concept of judgement, at the very least in a neutral sense, seems also to be inextricably linked with an after-life. It is not therefore necessary to propose, in Rabbi Lionel Blue's colourful turn of phrase, a cosmic concentration camp where God, the commandant, will torture souls for eternity because he loves them so much. If this notion is to be discarded, so also should be some of the prevalent sentimentality with regard to the details of the life beyond earthly existence. Any next life is a matter about which people must remain agnostic with regard to its content if not necessarily its existence.

This sentimentality is found, *par excellence*, in a passage of Henry Scott Holland's writings, for many years now a favourite at funerals, Christian and non-religious alike. Death is dismissed as 'nothing at all', and the deceased is to be thought of as in a room nearby, patiently waiting for a happy re-uniting with the bereaved in the near future. Even a familiar and more orthodox prayer which looks ahead to a 'joyful re-union in heaven' must be somewhat suspect, even if it is unquestionably consoling. One might certainly wish to give an affirmative answer to the question in the meltingly beautiful Eric Clapton song *Tears in Heaven* – 'Would it be the same, if you saw me in heaven?' Alas, we cannot give the answer we would wish, with integrity.

The Bible itself gives us no real sense of pattern to life beyond this. It seems that the idea of a life beyond death came into the Hebrew consciousness relatively late. In the time of Christ, it was still a matter of heated debate between Sadducees, who did not believe in a physical resurrection, and the Pharisees, who did. Jesus himself does not seem to have made a doctrine of life after death a central part of his teaching. He told parables which seem to pre-suppose a divine judgement at the end of earthly life. In reply to a trap question set by Sadducees, he suggested that marriage would not be part of a future life. The Easter-event was of course later presented as a hope for resurrection for Christ's followers, but the most prolific of the New Testament writers, St Paul, never succeeded in laying out a consistent blueprint for what he thought might lie beyond death. In his earlier writings (in particular the fifteenth chapter of the First Letter to the Corinthians) he seems to have been attached to the contemporary Jewish notions of a 'last day', when the dead would be raised and when judgement would take place. Later in his life, in his Letter to the Philippians, Paul seems to have come much closer to a more Hellenistic notion of life beyond death as a seamless transfer from one state of being to another, and he speaks simply of being with Christ when he dies. The later attempts in Christian history to provide detailed guide maps to heaven and of hell are, in every sense of that word, presumptuous.

But if we are to use the cipher of love as an explanation of some purpose to earthly life, does that point to the nature of a life beyond the earth? Many people clearly believe that it does, and we encounter, on a daily basis, anthropomorphisms where a casual assumption is made that heaven is essentially like earth, only better. Most people have had to endure funeral addresses where it is flippantly assumed that, in heaven, people go fishing and hold conversations, but where, presumably, there are no arguments and no rain.

Sometimes, however, this need for heaven to be like earth may be extremely moving in its expression. Charlotte Mew describes in her poem *Old Shepherd's Prayer* (which can be read properly , even to oneself, only in the accent of the English west country) an old shepherd dying in his room and hearing the sounds of farm work and animals outside. The shepherd concludes his prayer with the stanza

Heavenly Master, I would like to wake to they same green
   places
Where I be know'd for breaking dogs and follerin'
   sheep.
And if I may not walk in th' old ways and look on th' old
   faces
I wud sooner sleep.[2]

And it is probably true that all that would be 'required' of
heaven by most people is that it would resemble, as closely as
possible, the very best of earthly existence.

It is useful to look at the presuppositions behind some
much-loved poetry which touches on an after-life, and to
reflect on how they unquestionably resonate with the wish-
fulfilment for life as it has been known to continue beyond
death.

Some take a very different track to Charlotte Mew. In the
familiar *To His Coy Mistress*, Andrew Marvell is insistent that if
he and his beloved do not take action now as lovers, they will
have missed the opportunity for ever. He is clear that whatever
lies ahead will be only 'deserts of vast eternity'. Whatever may
be beyond the grave will, for Marvell, quite clearly not be as
pleasant as this life. Indeed, in death, the honour of the object
of his desire will turn to dust, as indeed will the poet's lust.

The grave's a fine and quiet place
But none, I think, do there embrace.[3]

In another, also much-anthologised poem, Elizabeth Barrett
Browning takes a more optimistic view. Rather than seeing
the next life as a place where human love ceases completely,
she entertains the hope that human love will there become
greater. In what has proved to be an all-time favourite as a

2. 'Old Shepherd's Prayer', *Praying with the English Poets* , 1990, London,
   Triangle, SPCK.
3. *Seventeenth Century Poetry*, 1996, Harmondsworth, Penguin Books.

poem of love, *How Do I Love Thee?*, she concludes the sonnet,

> ... I love thee with all the breath,
> Smiles, tears, of all my life! – And if God choose,
> I shall but love thee better after death.[4]

Leaving aside the question as to whether, for all their beauty, both Marvell's and Elizabeth Barrett Browning's ideas of love cross over a border into idolatry, there is an interesting contrast between both of them and the steely eye of Christina Rossetti. I believe that, if one only had the stern courage to embrace it, it is in Rossetti's attitude towards death that there is a more reasonable and sustainable response. Her *Song* presents the matter with a cool precision.

> When I am dead, my dearest,
> Sing no sad songs for me;
> Plant thou no roses near my head,
> Nor shady cypress tree.
> Be the green grass above me,
> With showers and dew-drops wet;
> And, if thou wilt, remember,
> And, if thou wilt, forget.
>
> I shall not see the shadows,
> I shall not feel the rain;
> I shall not hear the nightingale
> Sing on, as if in pain.
> But, dreaming through the twilight,
> That doth not rise nor set,
> Haply, I may remember,
> And, haply, may forget.[5]

Such agnosticism concerning the nature and content of an after-life, if not the possibility or even the probability of such

4. *Victorian Poetry*, 1996, Harmondsworth, Penguin Books.
5. *ibid.*

an existence, seems entirely appropriate. There is perhaps a useful *addendum* in the intensely unfashionable thought of judgement.

A God of judgement, as has already been suggested, is the God we love to despise. This image of God is so strong in much bad religion that we reject such a deity out of hand and regard ourselves as being very much more civilised for doing it. Such an attitude may well be civilised, but this does not prevent it also being totally flawed. Unless we are prepared to grapple – and grappling is what may well be involved – with a God who does actually care about what we are and what we do, and to whom ultimately we are answerable, then Christianity is a particularly futile and utterly inconsequential creed. As the American theologian Niebuhr put it in a famous phrase, it is belief in 'a God without wrath ushering a people without sin into a Kingdom without a cross'. We must still wrestle with the problem of how we can possibly even begin to relate to a God of judgement who is also a God of love, and therefore a God of forgiveness and of mercy.

It is not even slightly difficult to understand why there is such a distaste for any vision of God that would seek to terrorise people into belief. There is indeed a religion of spiritual terrorism that offers faith in Jesus Christ as an alternative to eternity in the fires of hell, these having been ignited personally by a God of infinite love. It is the basis for a populist evangelism that used to be a great deal more visible and audible than it is now in western society, although there are still remnants of it in some street-corner preaching.

But our intellect, coupled with our knowledge of the world in which we live with its huge diversity of cultures and of religious faiths, rebels instinctively against the simple idea that you might just hit the jackpot with the right faith and progress smoothly to eternal bliss or, on the other hand, be plain unlucky or invincibly ignorant of the right faith, and in consequence spend eternity in torment. Such an approach to religion would make the national lottery seem like a responsible investment policy for life savings.

There has also, throughout a century of vastly improved global communication, been the impact on the popular imagination of the sheer scale of the innocent suffering of millions of innocent people in wars, in famines and through incurable and horrifying disease. Perhaps the carnage of war has been the most decisive factor. There is indeed a very convincing argument that the crucial change in the conceptualisation of divine judgement came with the First World War. In the nineteenth and early twentieth centuries, religious people had no particular problems in accepting the reality of divine judgement as a concomitant to life beyond death. But the First World War was a crisis for that mode of thinking. When hundreds of thousands of young men were known to be dying in torment in the trenches of the Somme or the mud of Passchendale, it seemed obscene to assume that they had more anguish to face on the other side of death. And so a bizarre theodicy developed, that of Jesus as the great comrade waiting on the other side of death to welcome the boys home. (In fact, the lines of Henry Scott Holland, referred to earlier, with their image of death as nothing more than a transfer into another room, had their origins at this time.) There were, from this period onwards, fewer thoughts in the public religious imagination of a fearful judgement for anyone, even the most aggressive atheist. There was more than enough suffering in this life to believe that there could be any further discomfort for anyone in the next world.

At its most benign, people would now somehow expect God to be as lenient and tolerant as they themselves would be. The spirit of that famous supposed gravestone of Martin Elginbrodde would seem to sum the matter up more than adequately:

> Here lie I, Martin Elginbrodde,
> Ha' mercy on my soul, Lord Godde.
> As I would if I were Lord Godde,
> And thou wert Martin Elginbrodde.

As this century has progressed, this particular direction of argument has taken on a further dimension. For religious people today the question is: How could God dare to judge *anyone*, in view of all the unjust suffering in this world for which he should be considered responsible? In some ways this is a dangerous development, but it is one with which many people have to feel some sympathy. If you have to watch a friend die in pain and without dignity from a brain tumour or a cancer, you find yourself asking: How can any God have the gall to judge others who simply wouldn't ever do anything as dreadful as that to anyone?

The horrors of the Second World War – of an Auschwitz or a Belsen – have given a further momentum to this style of thinking. People now probably want God to answer for himself before they themselves can be expected to 'go on trial'. The answer that Job received in the Old Testament – that he had no right to question God if he took seriously the wonders and scale of creation – no longer seems to satisfy in the way it once did.

The effect has been that, even by devout Christian believers, less and less specific importance is given to life beyond this world. Much modern Christian theology is concerned with an encounter with this world, in terms of justice, of freedom, of care of the earth and of its people. Advent, traditionally the season of looking beyond death to the so-called 'last things', has been absorbed for the most part into Christmas festivity. In general terms, it is surely almost inconceivable that any contemporary hymn (as distinct from a secular song) would find much popularity if its theme was exclusively about the joys of heaven.

But can we then say that judgement is a necessary concept for any sense of individual existence beyond human death? Judgement seems to have a profound significance, not simply as part of biblical revelation, but because it is only in the context of a resolution beyond this world that this world has any meaning and structure. If we cannot conceive of anything other than this mortal existence, can there be any real coherence to existence here? It is certainly difficult, under any circumstances, to find any coherence in the cot-death, or the long drawn-out cancer or the death of the young mother. It is impossible to see any structure or meaning, if death is in fact the end of it all. Life of some nature beyond death, which would involve a straightening out of all the tangled threads of life here (and this must at least be a major part of what is meant by the judgement of God) is surely an essential if we are to find any shape in life or in faith. If whatever lies beyond this life is merely a seamless continuation of the same thing, or what Henry Scott Holland calls 'unbroken continuity', then religious belief and practice of any kind is a distraction from the business of real living. We might add that, from a specifically Christian perspective, any theology of the Cross as a place of reconciliation between God and humanity become redundant.

If we are therefore to see eternity and judgement as an essential framework to coherence and meaning in life, where do we go from there? In some ways, the shift in Christian thinking today towards the importance of life in this world is of considerable value. In the context of an eternity, life on earth is what is provided for humans so that each individual has the opportunity to become what God wants him or her to be. At death, we would hand back to God, for better, for worse, everything we have become in and through our living on earth, whatever that might be. Thus life, from beginning to end, is a constant preparation for death, but not in what might be dismissed as a pathologically melancholic way. For if life on earth is not somehow channelled (however falteringly) towards handing something worthwhile back to a God who gave us life, then it really would have very little direction. What the twentieth century perhaps tended to lose, with its insistent this-worldly perspective on faith, was a sense of purpose for being alive. This, in the context of some structure of eternity, would be the purpose of realising the potential of what God wills each of us to be, which (given that we are made differently in every sense) cannot be the same thing for everyone. Within this focus, life on earth becomes the constant location of future possibilities. A concept of judgement fits readily into this scheme of things. In fact it is at the very heart of any understanding that the end of a life on earth is a handing back to God of what has been made of what has been given. Judgement would therefore be a facing up to what we have become, and to what we could have become. In Emile Zola's phrase, only when all is known may all be healed.

How this might work itself out in eternity is beyond human speculation, as is the proposition that the dice of human destiny is cast in this life for all time. We may reasonably assume that we will each have to throw ourselves headlong at God's mercy and grace, trusting in love as well as justice. But at the end of it all, as has been said, we have no reason to believe that life beyond death is our human right, or something built in to creation itself. If it is there, it is a gift, a separate gift of God, and it is on his terms and not ours.

In a radio *Thought for the Day* a few years ago, a prison chaplain told of talking to a prisoner. The prisoner said that he felt he had more freedom than the chaplain, the warders or the prison governor, because he, the prisoner, had 'already been found out … ' Being found out, once and for all, might be a liberating experience, a shaming experience, a release. It would most probably be all three.

By way of an aside, we might also wonder whether part of the shame of being found out would be the realisation that we had made a fool of ourselves. In Dostoevsky's *The Devils* (in an appendix which was not part of the original novel), the principal character Stavrogin asks his confessor Tikhon if he should not make a public confession of a hideous sin in his earlier life. Tikhon warns him that, if he does so, it is not the hatred of the world he will encounter, but its mockery. 'The laughter,' he tells him, 'will be universal'. That, for Stavrogin, is perhaps the one thing he cannot face, and he leaves in despair.[6] To be laughed at may be a great deal more harrowing as a judgement than to be despised.

But we might consider a postscript in a New Testament parable of the talents. This is the familiar story of three men being entrusted with differing quantities of their master's belongings during his absence. Two invest the money, they both make one hundred percent profit for their master, and are commended equally for what they have done with their 'talents'. The third, given the smallest amount, simply preserves the money safely. He is condemned by his master. The parable is the reminder not only of accountability and judgement but also that 'safety first' is not the principle that Christ had in mind.

As a story it may well have been based on an earlier rabbinical parable where the three men used their money in three different ways. The first made a profit with the money and is commended. A second merely conserved his money and is commended slightly less. The only person who is punished is a third individual who has spent his master's money on orgies, extravagance and riotous living of every kind. In truth, most people would probably prefer that version, but Christ changes that scheme of things. He praises

---

6.  Fyodor Dostoevsky, *The Devils*, trans. David Magarshack, 1971, Harmondsworth, Penguin Books, pp. 701-4.

equally those who have done something positive, even at risk
(and a hundred per cent increase on any investment is not
only spectacular but very dangerous). There is condemnation
for the man who does nothing wrong but who takes no risks.
The actor Paul Eddington who died in 1995, said that he
wished his epitaph to be simply 'He did very little harm'.
Despite a genuine admiration for him, as an actor and as a
human being, I find this is somewhat less than the ideal as an
approach to Christian living.

There seems to be in Christ's teaching an invitation to
become everything that we could be in God's eyes, and that
must always be a matter of risk. What judgements would have
been delivered in the parable if the speculators had come
'unstuck' and, in trying to gain, had actually lost what they had
been lent? A reasonable hope is surely that they would not
have been given too harsh a judgement.

# 6

# The Twitching Curtain

How are we to relate to God? To put it more directly: how are we to speak to God and has this got anything to do with prayer? In which case, do prayers have either any meaning or any effect? The Welsh priest-poet R. S. Thomas in his poem *Folk Tale* uses the imagery of the Rapunzel fairy tale to give us a characteristically minimalist view of prayer –

> Prayers like gravel
>     Flung at the sky's
> window, hoping to attract
>         the loved one's attention. But without
>         visible plaits to let
> down for the believer
>     to climb up.
> To what purpose open
>     that far casement?
>         I would have refrained long since
>         but that peering once
> through my locked fingers
> I thought I detected
>     the movement of a curtain.[1]

In the Judeo-Christian tradition, attitudes to prayer, talking to God (or even at God), are diverse to the point of an apparent mutual exclusivity. There is a biblical tradition, particularly noticeable in the psalms, of metaphorically shaking one's fist at God. There are, however, other places in the Hebrew Scriptures where the only response to God is to throw oneself prostrate before him in humility. The prophet Job is ultimately forced into total submission. Both reactions seem

1.  R S Thomas, *Collected Poems*, 1993, London, Dent, p. 517.

appropriate. We are also, in both cases, talking about prayer. Prayer, however, cannot be considered outside a more general context of attitude to God.

There is a famous passage in Dostoevsky's *The Brothers Karamazov* where Ivan the atheist rounds on his gentle brother Alyosha, a former novice in the religious life, and suggests, more in tortured sorrow than in anger, that although God may exist, the price for the freedom God gives to us is unacceptable.[2] Ivan gives a number of harrowing examples of gratuitous cruelty to small children, where their pitiable cries for help from 'dear Father God' are ignored, and he then produces a savage denunciation of a world that can operate in such a way. No final and eternal harmonisation of what has been (and no requirement for human freedom, in order that such a harmonisation may occur) can, Ivan argues, justify the helpless cries of even one small child who is being tortured. The price is too high. 'Why recognise that devilish good-and-evil, when it costs so much? I mean, the entire universe of knowledge is not worth the tears of that little child addressed to "dear Father God".'

He also tells the story (quite possibly true) of a landowner, a retired General, who imprisons a young boy who has accidentally damaged one of his dogs. The next morning he releases the child but then sets his hounds on him. They hunt him down for sport and then the old General has his dogs tear the terrified little boy to pieces, right under the eyes of his mother. Now, says Ivan, forgiveness is just not possible in that situation. The mother has no right under any circumstances to forgive the General for what he has done nor to ask God to forgive him, because it was not done either to God or to her. Furthermore, nothing in the future, no 'prize' at the end of it all, no bliss in heaven for tortured children or anyone else,

2. Fyodor Dostoevsky, *The Brothers Karamazov,* trans. David Magarashack, 1982, Harmondsworth, Penguin, part ii, Book 5, section 4. p. 276 ff.

and no ultimate 'harmony', could ever make the torture of that one child worth the price for anyone, or even for everyone.

Ivan goes on to ask Alyosha a more demanding question. He asks whether if he, Alyosha, were designing the framework of human destiny, he could allow the possibility (or, even worse, the inevitability) of the torture of even one defenceless child in the name of freedom or anything else. No, says Ivan in answer to his own question, nothing could ever make it worthwhile, in this world or in the next. And so he remarks in a famous declaration, 'It is not God I do not accept, Alyosha. I merely most respectfully return him the ticket … '

But that cry of acute moral outrage against God is one to which the devout Alyosha simply cannot listen. Nor can he argue against it. All he can do is classify it as 'rebellion'. But it is in fact given a profound validity in the tormented words of Christ as he hangs on the cross in agony (to which reference has already been made in another context), 'My God, my God, why have you forsaken me?' Like Ivan Karamazov, but even less respectfully, Jesus Christ is *returning the ticket* to a 'dear Father God'.

So perhaps we not only may 'turn on God' at times, but we must turn on him if integrity is at stake. We may well want to find God 'guilty' for the way the world is, for the murder of children, or for what we believe he has done to us personally or to someone we love. And of course if we are less than honest about our real feelings, then we are doing ourselves no spiritual favours. But in finding God guilty, there is surely a strange reassurance in Christ's agonised and angry words from the cross. In those words there is a strange, barely to be grasped at, realisation that in that moment God, God in Christ, is somehow more the victim of all that is wrong in this world than are we.

There is here the strange affirmation that God is not

standing by, looking at the pain, but that he is inside it. God is not simply a witness, even a sympathetic witness, to the bitterness or sorrow. He is part of it. He is somehow not even outside our rejection of him, but is at the very centre of it with us. The paradox of the powerlessness of God gives a great deal more strength and comfort than any doctrine of his omnipotence. Returning the ticket is a necessity if a relationship with God is to retain integrity, and if the relationship, as anything other than words, is to survive. To pray with meaning is to engage with the deepest of human emotions and frustrations, including anger.

If it is permissible to be angry with God and to vent our frustration and disillusionment, can we say more about the individual responding to God. The Old Testament figure of Job presents a well-directed antithesis which deserves further attention at this point. The story is well known. Job, a good, upright and wealthy man, becomes the basis of a rather grotesque experiment (which God, incidentally, permits), to establish whether or not his attitude to God will change if he is the victim of hardship and tragedy. Various disasters befall, including bereavement, illness and financial ruin. His wife urges him to take the path that is even beyond the outburst of Christ – that he should 'curse God and die'. Job refuses and does not even blame God for his misfortunes. He has friends who try to explain the disasters in pious terms, suggesting, for example, that Job has clearly deserved what has happened to him. The consideration of the matter continues for chapter after chapter, but the *dénouement* comes when Job is forced to face the reality that if God is God, then he is so far beyond the comprehension of humanity that the only valid response can be submission.

There is a crucial reality that it is only when our rejection of God (if not of God's existence) is faced – and Ivan Karamazov's argument with Alyosha makes it quite clear that these are not the same thing – that the worship of God becomes a possibility which may be pursued with a real honesty. George Herbert's poem *The Collar* begins with rebellion and concludes with submission. His rebellion, it is true, is nearer to an urge to escape from God than the outright insurrection of Ivan Karamazov,

> I struck the board, and cried, No more
> I will abroad.
> What, shall I ever sigh and pine?
> My lines and life are free; free as the road,
> Loose as the wind, as large as store.
> Shall I still be in suit? [3]

And as the poet works his way through near-despair to the determination to be free of his 'collar', the sudden conclusion comes

> But as I raved and grew more fierce and wild
> At every word,
> Me thoughts I heard one calling, *Child!*
> And I replied, *My Lord.*

*The Collar* requires no elucidation, except perhaps a signal towards the penultimate line, 'Me thoughts I heard one calling … ' There is still no certainty, but there is a possibility.

What these brief excursions into Karamazov, Job and Herbert suggest is that rebellion may be necessary, and a necessary aspect of prayer, but that it cannot be sufficient in itself.

Rebellion, when it is combined with a belief in God, can easily become an intoxicating form of moral one-upmanship on God and, like many intoxicants, can become a drug in itself. It may seem that the only destinations of the rebellion against God are the alternatives of non-belief or submission.

---

3. George Herbert, *The Complete English Poems,* ed. John Tobin, 1991, Harmondsworth, Penguin.

Job, although angry and disillusioned, concludes in submission, as does Herbert. This perhaps implies that there is a single journey, and that once surrender is given, rebellion ceases to be a possibility. After all, Christ's suffering on the cross ends with words of surrender, 'Into your hands, I commit my spirit'. As with so much of what has been said hitherto in different settings, here again we have surely to live with a continuing tension, in this case a tension between rebellion and surrender: it is in that tension that truth and faith can find their place. What has been said of the way we speak of talking with God has an natural extension into how we think of prayer.

Any acceptance of the existence of a God who is accessible to individuals presents immediate questions on prayer, in particular what prayers should be like, and whether they do any good. Does a God who could intervene in the processes of nature and free-will ever choose to do so in response to prayer? It is certain that most prayer offered is intercessory, in some cases detailing requirements to be met by a benevolent deity, and it is here that we encounter the most outrageous distortions and presumptions. Most of us will know people who will claim that, as they drive into town, they always pray that a parking space may be available for them and who have never had that prayer, so to speak, 'turned down'. It is hard to know whether anything more misguided could be conceived. As we scarcely need reminding, if we are looking for an example of desperately sincere prayer, we need certainly look no further than the prayers of Jews who were being transported to Auschwitz. It is obscene to believe in a God who would turn down the desperate frightened prayers of children being dragged into gas chambers, and then find parking spaces for well-heeled motorists who are too lazy to walk for a few hundred yards, and pay a modest parking fee. For this could only mean one of two things. It might possibly mean that one has to have the line of communication to God exactly right, and that this involves membership of a particular religious institution, or the use of a particular choice of words. The alternative would seem to be that God is so capricious that he will intervene into the doings of the world for almost frivolous reasons, and remain distant from cries of suffering, fear and pain. If God needs his 'mind' changing by the insistence of those who have a clear line to him, he is scarcely worth belief. On a philosophical level, it certainly suggests that we cannot integrate omnipotence, omniscience and perfect love in one single Being.

If there is a purpose in prayer, even intercessory prayer, it can surely be only to bring the mind and heart of the supplicant into conformity with the will of God. There is good reason to be suspicious of the rigid distinctions between thanksgiving, intercession and adoration. The purpose and the motivation of all prayer should be the same. This does not exclude anger as a component at times for if there is dialogue, even with raised voices, there is at least relationship. Where anger is unacknowledged, the anger becomes deeply destructive.

There is a useful paradigm of this in the New Testament story of the call to the Blessed Virgin Mary. She is told that she is to be the mother of the Christ. Her response, as is well known, is surrender to God's will after initial misgiving. And so the first part of the prayer response to any turn of events beyond our control may well be to ask that, in the spiritual realm at least, we may (in the words of an old Beatles song), 'Let it be', or as Mary in the New Testament story actually says, 'May it be as you have said'. That may often be the most difficult journey any individual has to make. It must have been for Mary. There was the prospect of shame and of pain, and, further ahead (if she could see that far) the prospect of separation and, ultimately, of witnessing the violent death of this child now being foisted upon her. 'Letting it be' would have been a costly acceptance.

It may be a long journey to that point, as an individual faces illness, whether in themselves or in someone about whom they care. As one looks down a barrel of separation, aliena-tion, treachery, unemployment, alone-ness, or unpopularity, an almost inevitable reaction is anger: 'Why should this happen?' 'Why me?' 'What have I done to deserve this?'

We should not suppose, either, that anger was absent from Mary's initial response. Her first words, 'How can this be?' probably meant 'This is absurd' or 'This is unfair', if not a blank denial. Elizabeth Kübler Ross, in her famous treatment of the sequence of events in the human response to terminal illness or bereavement, places anger very near the beginning of the sequence, very shortly after denial. There is first a denial: 'There's been a mistake', 'There's been a mix-up – it's someone else … ' Then comes the anger, a natural anger with everyone including God, and perhaps particularly with God. Letting it be is a long way down the road. Very often it is the last step on the road, an acceptance of what is to come, regardless of what that future may be, good or bad. Many people never get that far. Events overtake them. There is only anger and nothing beyond it, and this can be true of prayer. But yet although the story of Mary is a reminder that the path must take us to acceptance, to letting it be, it is a reminder also that the same road should take us further.

To see this further stage, perhaps we should move from those icons of the 60s, the Beatles, to an icon of the 1990s, *Star Trek*'s Jean-Luc Picard. Probably Picard's best-known catch phrase is 'Make it so … ' In other words, somewhere there has to be a movement from the passive and the 'accepting', to the active and the constructive. And so Mary's acceptance of her situation moves on, moves forwards into the victory of what is known as the *Magnificat* with its determined rallying-cry, 'My soul magnifies the Lord ... he has shown strength with his arm ... he has scattered the proud in the imagination of their hearts ... he has thrown down the mighty from their seats ... he has exalted the humble and meek'. This is a song of militancy and challenge, not against God, but against injustice and corruption. It is a proclamation of divine victory: 'Make it so ... ' Consequently there is in prayer, at its best and most effective, a journey from the passive to the active, from acceptance that some things will be as they will be, to a willingness to be an active part of the pattern of God's future.

If prayer is in some way to have meaning, it must be something that affects the pray-er, even if little else is changed. This does not necessarily mean that events will not be changed as the result of prayer, but we can assume that generally it will be more through God-directed human activity than by divine miraculous intervention. There may be a genuine objective miracle: divine interference in the standard course of nature clearly cannot be beyond God's capability? But have we the right to expect it? There would be something profoundly immoral if R.S. Thomas' window in the sky opened when the gravel had come from the right source and with the right aim, whereas the curtain would not even twitch if the thrower were not sufficiently talented to throw accurately.

Thus far, much of what has been said about relating to God has been talking at God. That can only be the most immature mode of prayer, even if it is its most natural. Two other aspects must be mentioned, both of them demanding, although neither implies any insistence that we see a curtain twitching in the sky.

The first is the place of silence and nothingness in prayer, what Christian spiritual writers know as solitude. If we think of prayer as, in some way, a relationship with God, then silence should be a reasonable part of that relationship. After all, when we are alone with a real friend, there is no great demand

that we babble away in conversation in order to ensure that
the friendship is secure. The contrary is often true. It is only
with those with whom we are at ease that silence seems
unthreatening and soothing. Solitude with God may not be as
soothing, and certainly not in the early stages. A great modern
guru of Christian spirituality, the late Henri Nouwen, rightly
draws our attention to the difference between solitude and
privacy.

> In order to understand the meaning of solitude, we must
> first unmask the ways in which the idea of solitude has
> been distorted by our world. We say to each other that we
> need some solitude in our lives. What we really are
> thinking of, however, is a time and a place for ourselves
> in which we are not bothered by other people, can think
> our own thoughts, express our own complaints, and do
> our own thing, whatever it may be. For us, solitude most
> often means privacy. We have come to the dubious
> conviction that we all have a right to privacy. Solitude
> thus becomes like a spiritual property for which we can
> compete on the free market of spiritual goods. But there
> is more. We also think of solitude as a station where we
> can recharge our batteries, or as the corner of the
> boxing ring where our wounds are oiled, our muscles
> massaged, and our courage re' stored by fitting slogans.
> In short, we think of solitude as a place where we gather
> new strength to continue the ongoing competition in
> life.
>
> Solitude is not a private therapeutic place. Rather, it
> is the place of conversion, the place where the old self
> dies and the new self is born, the place where the
> emergence of the new man and the new woman occurs.
>
> In solitude I get rid of my scaffolding: no friends to
> talk with, no telephone calls to make, no meetings to
> attend, no music to entertain, no books to distract, just

me – naked, vulnerable, weak, sinful, deprived, broken
– nothing: It is this nothingness that I have to face in my
solitude, a nothingness so dreadful that everything in
me wants to run to my friends, my work, and my distrac-
tions so that I can forget my nothingness and make
myself believe that I am worth something.[4]

If we cannot face that type of solitude, we are refusing to
face either ourselves or God. It is only in facing the nothingness that a sense can emerge of the something that is true, real
and beyond us.

The second is the place of routine and rhythm in prayer. In
many Christian traditions there is the tradition, not simply of
praying every day but of daily set prayer. It is appropriate that
it should in the western Christian tradition have been known
through the centuries as the Office, with all those associations
added today of a place of work and a routine. The discipline
of the daily set prayer, with all that it brings in a spiritual
routine, may very easily be dismissed by cynics as a form of
hypnotic suggestion. It is of course impossible, as with so many
other things, to disprove such a claim. What is, however,
certain is that for thousands upon thousands of people (and
not merely clergy) it has been the mainstay of a relationship
with the other, even when all the other intellectual and
emotional props seem to have disappeared.

The discipline of the daily set prayer can never be the
totality. It may, however, be the sustenance of relationship
which carries the pray-er through a no-man's land of vulnerability, loss of faith and what the mediaeval writers called
*accidie*, the dryness of spirit that brings the individual to the
edge of blackness and despair. It is perhaps only through the
locked fingers of a prayer of routine that we see with relief the
twitching of the curtain.

4. From *The Way of the Heart*, by Henri Nouwen, published and copyright
   1992 by Darton Longman and Todd Ltd and used by permission of the
   publishers.

# 7

# Games Churches Play

There are some truisms which, for all that they have become *cliché*, cannot safely be discounted. It is such a truism that one of the primary obstacles to religious belief is the public face of religious institutions – in the case of Christian belief, the Christian Church. It may of course be argued that the Church is, at very least, a necessary evil. Faith can only be communicated by the Church in its broadest sense, the Church as a collection of believing people. It is, however, the *appearance* of believing people organised that causes particular difficulties for the sensitive onlooker. It is at times indeed difficult to believe that an institution which has all the appearance of human corruption can be the eternal bearer of either beauty or truth.

The ways in which the Church and individual Churches have developed must take a major responsibility. Because the individual Churches are organisations (no matter how divine we may regard their foundation or origins), human craving for power and for personal and corporate aggrandisement come into play. Very speedily, all that is visible of the Church to the outsider is the demand for power. And with the pursuit of power come divisions and divisiveness. If the Church were to have the courage to be truthful about itself, it would also accept that the divisions and divisiveness have prevented men and women in their millions from seeing any worthwhile reality behind the externals. The politicisation of the Church and the *modus operandi* of the Churches as a series of power-bases have together combined to hide the basic message of Christianity from the intelligent and critical onlooker. In short, Christ has been successfully hidden behind obsessively manipulative structures.

Thinking of the nature of the Church's relationship with that which is outside it, there is a further difficulty. The Church may reasonably be described as resembling a ghetto. At its most powerful, it is a large ghetto that has invited whole nations to enter within its walls, but it has remained a ghetto. At its politically weakest, it was a ghetto which clung to its individual identity, regardless of a world beyond. Perhaps this image requires further elaboration.

The Italian writer Primo Levi was remarkable as one of the only survivors of Auschwitz who could write of his experiences calmly and even compassionately. He certainly could not forgive those who had perpetrated the Holocaust, but then he could not really forgive himself either for having survived the concentration camps. He could, however, speak gently and, in places, even dispassionately of those who, he says, cannot simply and smugly be stereotyped as monsters. They were, he says, 'made of our same cloth, they were average human beings, averagely intelligent, averagely wicked: save for exceptions, they were not monsters, they had our faces ... '[1]

In this last book, *The Drowned and the Saved,* Levi tells the story of Chaim Rumkowski who was made 'President' of the Jewish ghetto in Lodz in Poland.[2] A man of around sixty in 1940, a small industrialist, he was put in charge by the Nazis of running the local ghetto. Never having had much power until then, Rumkowski used his delegated dictatorship with great *élan.* He obtained authorisation to print money, there were stamps with his face on them, he wore royal clothes and, in every sense, Rumkowski 'held court'. He also had a highly efficient police force to guard his 160,000 subjects and, all in all, he ran the place rather well. But all good things come to an end, and in 1944, the Lodz ghetto was liquidated. Rumkowski, to mark his status, was even allowed to travel to

1. Primo Levi, *The Drowned and the Saved,* 1989, London, Abacus, p. 169.
2. *Ibid.* pp. 43-51.

Auschwitz in his own special private limousine. But, then, with his 'subjects', he was put into a gas chamber ...

Levi points out that such a story cannot be self-enclosed. It encapsulates the entire theme of what he calls 'the grey zone'. Rumkowski is a symbolic figure of a band of 'half-consciences'. But, Levi asks, how solid a moral armature does anyone have? How would each of us behave if driven by necessity, or lured by the seduction of power? 'No,' says Levi, 'we too are so dazzled by power and prestige as to forget our essential fragility: willing or not we come to terms with power, forgetting that we are all in the ghetto, that the ghetto is walled in, that outside the ghetto reign the lords of death, and that close by the train is waiting ... '[3]

For Levi, the ghetto is simply the place which can be self-contained and which believes itself to be self-contained. It may well be moral and orderly after a fashion. After all, the Lodz ghetto from within was no worse as a system than a thousand others. The ghetto is a place where moral judgements, even judgement itself, can comfortably be suspended, because we choose to forget that the ghetto is in thrall to the lords of death and that, close by, the train is waiting.

The Church through history has had many of the comfortable aspects of ghetto. It has had its authority structure, not necessarily very corrupt, but with all the characteristics of a self-contained system which does not really engage with that which allows it to exist only because it is no trouble. If the Church cannot engage with an uncomfortable world that will inevitably change it, then it will only ever be a ghetto, on however large or small a scale.

A second issue which has also insidiously damaged the Church through the centuries has been its attitude to sanctity. There has been an unfortunate assumption that holiness and moral perfection are coterminous. No one is likely to suggest

3. *Ibid.* pp. 50-51.

that holiness and moral uprightness are utterly disconnected from each other. But the Church has too often misunderstood and misrepresented the meaning of holiness in suggesting to the world that religious people will inevitably be 'better' people than those who have no faith.

Holiness does not make people extraordinarily good, and even less does it make them morally perfect. Holiness refers in its origins to an apartness – but not in the sense of ghetto, more in the understanding that a focus on life is different. St Paul can describe the Corinthians as those called to be saints (or holy), and then reasonably lacerate them for every kind of failing and sin. Holiness is not perfection. If we consider the New Testament saints for even a few moments that would be obvious. St Paul could be very unforgiving and very conscious of his own suffering for the Gospel. St Peter could be indecisive and at times downright cowardly, even after the resurrection. Matthew and Simon the Zealot, politically, had no common ground with one another. In a parallel context of an occupied country during the Second World War, Matthew would have been termed a quisling, and Simon a resistance fighter. Saints of history are not only varied but also imperfect.

The consequences of suggesting that deep religious faith and moral goodness are almost synonymous has been more than misleading. They have been disastrous. Certainly moral misbehaviour will call into question the depth of religious adherence, but we must be careful not to assume the converse. There is a familiar story of Evelyn Waugh who, when he was upbraided for being generally unpleasant and was asked how he could square his unpleasantness with his Catholic faith, replied simply that he would have been a great deal worse if he had not had his faith. Now certainly a believer should commend his or her faith by actions, but there are particular dangers in presenting religious allegiance as an automatic improver of behaviour. Much of the gloating en-

gendered in recent years by clerical scandals in Britain and
Ireland have their origins in the culture of a moral caste
system, the assumption that clergy will be more moral and
generally better people than the laity. It is a mind-set which
the clergy themselves have never properly discouraged. And,
at a more general level, one cannot seriously impugn Cupitt's
attack on the Church as it is experienced by many.

> The Church believes in a Gospel of grace and forgive-
> ness but it doesn't act forgiven. Too often it is irritable,
> querulous, censorious, inhibited and depressive, exces-
> sively self-conscious, and apt to use moral superiority
> and spiritual power over others.[4]

If, therefore, one may see the behaviour of the Church as
occasioning problems in believing, how necessary is the
Church? There is an obvious and facile answer that the
Church, either as community or even as a collection of
persons, is the sole means by which the content of the
Christian Gospel survives through the generations.

The question therefore needs to be re-phrased. If it is
necessary to have some organised means for continuing a
proclamation of Christianity, is there any need for either a
structured 'ordained' ministry or formalised sacraments, both
of which readily become pretexts for power-play? Many Christians, including many Trinitarian Christians, would reply in
the negative. Without deviating into a full-scale ecclesiology
of either ministry or sacraments, it may be said simply that an
embryonic form of an authorised ministry is apparent from
the earliest days of Christianity, and the same may be said for
an understanding of sacraments as visible signs of a grace
thereby imparted . The notion that one may go a great deal
further and un-church other believers on the grounds that
they have not got the formula or the terminology exactly right

4. Don Cupitt, *The New Christian Ethics*. London, SCM, p. 68

– in other words, the same formula or terminology as we have
– is simply a return to the power games referred to earlier in
this chapter. It would be naïve to imagine that any structure,
even a structure organised to achieve good ends, will not seek
to defend itself, and thereby run the risk of becoming an end
and a destination in itself. But the failures of the organisation
of the Church in certain areas is not a justification for either
neurosis or paralysis.Rather they call for a sense of propor-
tion. The Church, even at its worst, is somehow the bearer of
God.

To return to the image of ghetto, the most important task
for the Church of today is the removal of its metaphorical
walls. There is a phrase in the Old Testament book, Zechariah,
'Run and say to that young man, "Jerusalem shall be inhabited
as villages without walls".' Being Church can never be effective inside walls. And therein lies the huge risk. Whatever else
the Christian faith is, it should be – for the Church in all its
aspects – a matter of danger and certainly of uncertainty and
adventure. These may not necessarily be the most pleasant of
adventures, but there should always be on the Church's
agenda a series of new understandings, sometimes new qualms,
sometimes new insights, new certainties – rather than final
conclusions. When the Church reaches the place where it
reckons that everything has now been worked out, or is other
than provisional, then it is already dead in everything but
name.

The image throughout Scripture is of people moving –
moving bodily from Egypt to Canaan, moving in and out of
exile, moving from Bethlehem to Jerusalem, moving on
missionary journeys through the known world, but moving
forwards spiritually as well. Peter's understanding of Christ
grew and grew, from his own unpromising beginnings as an
egocentric and unpredictable bully who was called by Jesus on
the shores of Galilee. And part of the proper vocation of the

Church is therefore to retain the ability to move and to change.

Being a city that does not need walls for its protection means that the Church is never to shirk, whether through fear or through laziness, the task of thinking through the spiritual, social and political implications of life on earth. In other words, the Church must be unafraid to admit that it does not have every answer. It must at least square up to the hard questions of life, whether on the one hand the intensely personal question: 'Why should that child have died if there is a God of love?' Or, equally, the political question: 'Why should we live in a world where, every other second, a child dies needlessly of starvation or disease, while we still destroy food and are paid for doing it?' There are honest searching questions which will not guarantee the popularity of the Church in the houses of commerce or of parliament. But the refusal to ask such questions will lose the Church credibility as it cowers in its ghetto of respectability and safety.

One of the temptations to which the Church has succumbed over centuries has been the tendency to airbrush out of the biblical picture of the Incarnation aspects which would make the Church appear dangerous to secular rule. Any detached reading of the biblical picture of Christ (in particular the picture presented in the Gospel of Luke) would insist that he had a particular bias, even favouritism, to those who are outside the circle of respectability. Many of the stories in Luke point to the particular concern of Christ to include those who, either because they are women or gentiles or regarded as quislings by the majority of people, were denied proper membership of their own society. For Jesus Christ, as portrayed by Luke in particular, the outsiders assume more importance than the insiders.

This insight has long since been successfully removed from the middle-class western view of what the Church is to be and

to say. The Church has been interested in outsiders only so
that they may become insiders, and under its authority. We
have traditionally devoted a great deal of our energies into
deciding who is inside our walls and who is outside. Some of
this has been the pursuit of control. Some has had to do with
the requirement for support, in particular financial support.
Some has been in the name of orthodoxy. And yet it seems
probable that in the western society of today, a majority of
people who would centre their lives (albeit in some cases
rather vaguely) on the precepts of Christ have no affiliation
with any Christian community. They are believing outsiders
who have no wish to be insiders for as long as the Church will
recognise them only as membership fodder.

Above all else, in western culture, the Church rarely chal-
lenges the social or economic *status quo*, probably less in fear
of persecution from the outsider than of the disaffection of
the insider, This becomes particularly obvious during the
western celebration of Christmas. There are aspects of the
Christmas stories (however we may understand those narra-
tives historically) which, if they were read dispassionately,
would shriek at the actuality of much modern society. There
is an account of a massacre of children. It is reckoned that
following the Gulf War in 1991, over half a million children
died in Iraq as a direct result of the sanctions which were
supposedly to keep Saddam Hussein on a leash. And that
figure of half a million was not Iraqi propaganda. It came from
the United Nations Food and Agriculture Organisation. In
October 1996, it was reckoned by UNICEF that over fifty per
cent of women and children in Iraq were receiving less than
half their calorific needs. In less clinical language, they were
starving to death. Somehow the western Church seems able to
read the story of Christmas and relegate the slaughter of the
innocents to the level of pantomime.

The vision presented by liberation theology, itself in many

respects at its own crossroads today, seems a universe away from the setting of a cosy and comfortable western Church. Yet the cosiness and comfort of the westernised Church becomes visibly more an object of pity and contempt as the years pass, and as the tide of western faith-culture ebbs. We can no longer ignore the foundation on which liberation theology in its earlier and more exciting years (now more than a generation ago) was constructed. Here is the absolute certainty that the God of Scripture and of Christ sides with the oppressed against those who oppress, whether physically or economically. Indeed, as the liberation theologians reminded the world, one of the names for God in the Hebrew Scriptures is *Go'el*, a word which means 'he who achieves justice for those who are weak'.

In western society, where the mainstream Churches are still surviving on the after-burn of Christendom – that vast tract of history where Church and state belonged to one another – such comments are still in the arena of *cliché* and posture. This will indeed change. It will not only be the few brave and seemingly eccentric souls who will enunciate the choice that must be made between God and mammon, between *Go'el* and the culture of 'devil take the hindmost'. The Incarnation is at its heart the tale of *Go'el* in Christ, taking on oppression and suffering the ultimate oppression of judicial torture and murder, so that love and mercy, not simply in the future but in the present, might be brought into reality. The proclamation of the Kingdom of God – the ruling of God – cannot be done from within the illusionary protective walls of the ghetto, or from beneath the parapet of a trench. Only when the Church as a whole is, by its very being, a challenge to the injustice that perpetuates misery (to the degree that in consequence of its effrontery the Christian community itself becomes a figure of scorn and hatred) can it ever regain its credentials as the Body of Christ.

Avoiding the temptation to deflect into a sacramental theology which is certainly not part of the intended structure of this book, it should nevertheless be said that only if we try to earth the notion of a sacrament in the life of the world outside, rather than in the sanctuary of the church building, can the link between sacraments as rite and sacraments as reality become clear, and the life of the Church take on its coherence.

Christ's life was itself a sacrament, 'showing' and 'doing', in demonstrating the fullness of love, and in effecting a reconciliation in the no-man's land of the cross. The Church itself is to be conceptually a sacrament, showing the meaning of Christ and doing the work of Christ. And the rites of Eucharist and baptism are sacraments, earthed in the life of Christ and the life of the Church. To reduce them to magic in the sanctuary is to make a absurdity both of Christ and of the Church. But, paradoxically, the sacramental life of the Church is precisely why the Church has to be taken seriously as God-bearer. This can only happen when the Church, as the Swiss theologian Hans Urs von Balthasar has put it, 'lies open to the world'[5] Otherwise, all that is left is the wholly formalised, the hierarchical organisation, which, as he says, can only appear superfluous if not totally lacking in credibility.

The Church must therefore always be in the process of risking its survival, and thus living outside the walls of the ghetto. Any community functions best as real community when it works for a focus beyond itself and its own continuance. The Christian community is at its most effective when it is not feverishly plotting its own survival, but is functioning unselfconsciously for an end beyond itself and its survival. That is, by any calculation, what the over-used word *mission* actually means.

5. Hans Urs Von Balthasar, *Engagement with God*, 1975, London, SPCK, pp. 17-19.

# 8

# Virtuous Unreality

In one of her longer poems, *How do you see?*, Stevie Smith urges the importance of learning 'to be good without enchantment'. She herself undoubtedly existed in an uncertain world, perhaps another no-man's land, a place between disgusted belief and reluctant unbelief. An old friend once wrote of her that she was neither a believer, an unbeliever nor agnostic, but all three at the same time, who 'did not like the God of Christian orthodoxy, but she could not disregard Him or ever quite bring herself to disbelieve in Him.' [1]

In that poem she raises the crucial question as to whether one needs what she calls 'enchantment', which we may presumably take as God or religion, in order to have goodness. She clearly thinks not, but goes further in suggesting that if humanity cannot soon grasp the notion of virtue without religion (and without Christianity in particular), the results will be catastrophic. Conceding that Christianity is kinder than it once was, but that this is also true of colonial systems, which also tend to become kinder but only before they disappear, she muses as to whether Christianity should not now vanish, for the good of all ...

> I do not think we shall be able to bear much longer the dishonesty
> Of clinging for comfort to beliefs we do not believe in
> For comfort, and to be comfortably free of the fear
> Of diminishing good, as if truth were a convenience.
> I think if we do not learn quickly, and learn to teach children
> To be good without enchantment, without the help

1. Stevie Smith, *Selected Poems*, ed. James MacGibbon, 1978, Harmondsworth, Penguin Books, p. 19. Copyright estate of James MacGibbon.

Of beautiful painted fairy stories pretending to be true,
Then I think it will be too much for us, the dishonesty
And, armed as we are now, we shall kill everybody,
It will be too much for us, we shall kill everybody. [2]

On this reckoning, therefore, goodness in moral terms is based at present on a system of what we might usefully describe as unbelieved beliefs, a structure of 'beautiful painted fairy-stories' which give goodness its context in enchantment, but which are in reality untrue, unnecessary, and now even downright dangerous. Don Cupitt underlines this line of argument in philosophical thought, suggesting from his earliest writings that autonomy is crucial to our being, and that any moral structure we employ should be one which has been generated within ourselves, and not 'an objective ready-made framework' [3] in which to live our lives.

In a later point of this book, *Taking Leave of God*, Cupitt posits a Christianised Buddhism which, for him, suggests something that is clearly a 'good without enchantment'. So, he suggests,

it is good that one should appraise oneself and one's life with an unconditional religious seriousness that tolerates no concealment or self-deception ... It is good that one should come to transcend the mean defensive ego and learn absolute disinterestedness and purity of heart. [4]

But is one not reasonably left with an honest 'Why?' to such concepts of virtue in the absence of an objective framework. In other words, Why, precisely, is it good to have a seriousness of purpose in life? Why should we believe it is good to overcome an ego, however enormous? If we return to the brutal firmness of Ivan Karamazov's intellectual atheism, we

2. *Selected Poems.*
3. Don Cupitt, *Taking Leave of God*, 1980, London, SCM Press, p. 3.
4. *Ibid.* p. 82.

find a point of view which runs totally counter to Cupitt. In a scene in the monk Zosima's cell, Karamazov's kinsman Miusov outlines this thesis with a commendable brevity: Ivan, he announces had said

> that there was nothing in the whole law of nature that man should love mankind, and that, if there had been any love hitherto, it was not owing to a natural law, but simply because men believed in immortality. Ivan Fyodorovich added in parentheses that the whole natural law lies in that faith, and that if you were to destroy in mankind the belief in immortality, not only love but every living force maintaining the life of the world would at once be dried up. Moreover, nothing then would be immoral, everything would be lawful, even cannibalism. And that's not all. He ended by asserting that for every individual, like ourselves, who does not believe in God or immortality, the moral law of nature must immediately be changed into the exact contrary of the former religious law and that egoism, even to crime, must become not only lawful but even recognised as the inevitable, the most rational, even honourable outcome of his position.[5]

It is of course one of the brilliant ironies of the great novel that Ivan Karamazov cannot quite sustain this position consistently in his own life, at either a practical or an emotional level, but is instead beset by every kind of high-minded scruple of conscience. But this does not in itself alter the reality that a *prima facie* case against his argument cannot readily be adduced. And there is a crucial subtlety in the fact that Ivan does not speak of punishment or judgement as the basis for morality, but only of immortality.

5.  Fyodor Dostoevsky, *The Brothers Karazamov* trans.David Magarshack, 1982, Harmondsworth, Penguin Books,  pt.i, Book 2, section 6, p. 77.

If the argument for morality were based only on fear of divine punishment in some after-life, it would be considerably weakened, because if morally good behaviour is only for the avoidance of pain in an after-life, it has more to do with prudence than with morality. Goodness, if it is truly good, must have an altruism attached to it. What Karamazov is suggesting is far more refined than the mere escape from divine wrath. He is proposing that morality must have a context beyond the visible and tangible. If the activity of neurones within us has no extrinsic significance, or any connection with some objective framework beyond themselves (the type of framework that a Cupitt or a Stevie Smith would wish us to reject), then the same neurones would certainly be better employed providing us with pleasure.

May one in fact argue, then, within an entirely mechanical view of human self-consciousness, that morality has any meaning? By this I mean whether one may indeed have good without enchantment, or (to tinker with computer jargon) have a 'virtuous unreality' – virtue in the context of a God or an enchantment that is not real?

Let us therefore assume, for the sake of the argument, that humanity is not connected to anything beyond itself. We may certainly see why there should be a regulatory pattern to community existence. Individuals who do not conform to whatever is for the survival (or even the comfort) of the group should be removed, either temporarily or permanently, in the interests of the group, so that damage to the greater number may be minimised. This is all logical but has absolutely nothing to do with morality, which has at least something to do with Cupitt's suggestion that it is good to transcend the mean, defensive ego. It seems certain that the only reason to impose any self-discipline on the ego in such a situation would be to avoid punishment by the group under its regulations if one breaks its code, or else, more subtly, to avoid ostracisation by the group which will marginalise (socially if not legislatively) any individual ego it considers to be overactive. In which case, the individual should simply learn to operate in such a way as will engender the greatest comfort (which may well include a degree of popularity) for the selfish ego, and to avoid the greatest discomfort (which would certainly include punishment and social isolation) for the selfsame ego if it were to aggravate the other egos around it. To do otherwise is in no sense immoral, but merely foolish or pathological.

Yet it appears from observation – and perhaps from experience also – that one may indeed seek to overcome ego in response to the love of another human being. But if that love is itself disconnected from anything other than a particular bombardment of neurones, themselves perhaps stimulated by visual or olfactory stimuli, there seems little value in the exercise. It would be wiser to fake unselfish love, and instead to work clinically for the desired object of the enterprise, leaving one's ego in its existing unreformed state. Eating, drinking, and being merry (albeit deviously in order to avoid social ostracisation) because the neurones will at some stage, and certainly in death, cease their dancing, seems a more profitable use of time and energy.

But none of this seems to answer the basic problem. After all, even if there seems to be no compelling reason for good without enchantment, that does not itself establish that because there seems to be unselfish good around there therefore has to be enchantment. This was certainly hinted at by Kant when he saw at least a logic for God's existence by the presence of what he believed was an objective 'moral law within', which he would have argued was not simply within but also built-in.

If, however, we return to the Dawkinsesque picture of the selfish gene – humanity as concerned only with survival – we are still left puzzled. Dawkins carries the model of the selfish

gene further and suggests that ideas can be transmitted
through human bodies down the generations, again to secure
the survival of the species. These genetic memories he calls
'memes'. Presumably Kant's 'moral law within' would come
within the range of meme behaviour. Yet, for humankind to
have built such an enormous panoply of apparent morality
and a system of in-built notions of unselfish altruism simply in
order to survive looks like rather extensive over-elaboration.
It has to be said that evolutionary biologists might not necessarily accept this line of argument. Nearly thirty years ago, the
concept of reciprocal altruism was suggested by the biologist
Robert Trivers. This was, in basic terms, the idea that animals
may well do favours for other animals because they expect that
the good turn will be repaid at some stage. But this is certainly
a misuse of the term 'altruism', which cannot be altruism if it
expects the 'generosity' to be reciprocated.

The biologist Matt Ridley has argued forcefully that gene-
survival is everything, and that the motivation to continue the
species (and in good order) will make anything from ants
upwards do apparently unselfish things for the sake of the
common good. Drawing on the researches of William Hamilton, Ridley points out that the ant's unselfishness is geared to
the species' survival.

All sorts of behaviour that had seemed puzzling when
seen through the lens of the individual or the species,
suddenly became clear when seen through a gene-
focused lens. In particular, as Hamilton triumphantly
showed, the social insects, by helping their sisters to
breed, left more copies of their genes in the next
generation than by trying to breed themselves. From the
gene's point of view therefore, the astonishing altruism
of the worker ant was purely, unambiguously selfish.
The selfless co-operation of the ant colony was an illu-
sion: each worker ant was striving for genetic eternity

through its brothers and sisters, the queen's royal offspring, rather than through its own offspring, but it was
doing so with just as much gene-selfishness as any human being elbowing aside his rivals on the way up the
corporate ladder.[6]

At one level, it is impossible to say that Ridley is wrong in
extrapolating the logic of this to human behaviour, and it is
far too facile to say that the ant's selfish unselfishness is not
based on conscious decision, whereas the human being who
chooses the sacrificial and unselfish path is making a conscious and therefore a conscientious decision. After all, we do
not know exactly how 'unconscious' an ant is and, in any case,
Ridley would instantly retort that gene-selfishness is sufficiently sophisticated to make us imagine that we are taking a
free unselfish action. Our sense of freedom of choice in an
apparently unselfish act, it could be argued, is itself a gene-
implanted delusion.

Again, as with Dawkins, this is a philosophical rather than
a strictly scientific judgement. He is entitled to make such a
judgement, but not to call it empirical fact. We who are inside
the machine cannot be entirely sure as to how and why the
machine works the way it does. An action which is rash but
sacrificial may seem to one observer to be pathological. To
another observer, equally detached, it is altruism of the most
noble kind.

But we have still to ask what may be the basis of good with
enchantment. We may go down the road avoided assiduously
by Ivan Karamazov, and suggest that we are good on earth in
order to avoid divine torture in the hereafter. Not only does
Karamazov deny the avoiding of possible dispatch to hell as a
basis for morality, but a principal reason for his denial of God
as a moral being is that divine reconciliation and forgiveness

6.   Matt Ridley, *The Origins of Virtue*, 1997, Harmondsworth, Penguin Books,
     p. 18.

even of the unforgivable appear to him to be an integral part of the package of eternal salvation. In any case, to be good for the avoidance of punishment or the receipt of reward can, as has already been suggested, only be prudence masquerading as morality.

The famous prayer attributed to Ignatius of Loyola has a phrase which is often disregarded, probably because of the sheer enormity of what it is saying: the supplicant asks 'to labour and not to ask for any reward save that of knowing that we do Thy will'. The only clear basis for genuine good because of enchantment can surely be as response to divine will or, in the case of Christianity, divine love. It was suggested earlier in this chapter that to seek to overcome the ego and natural selfishness, in response to the human love of another, is neither necessary nor laudable, if human love has no connection with an objective, prior, and transcendent love. If human love does, however, have a context in a larger framework, then a reasonable response will be the overcoming of selfishness. We may go further and argue that if our very existence is based on a fundamental love or unselfishness in God, then a proper human reaction should be the emulation of that love in the overcoming of the self's natural impulses.

It seems helpful now to return to Cupitt, but in a more positive frame of mind, and to two sections in his writing, the second far more recent that the first.

In his seminal *Taking Leave of God* Cupitt suggested that 'obedience to a good God is only meritorious in so far as I freely and rationally judge for myself that God's commands are intrinsically good, so that I could choose to obey them in any case whether God commanded them or not'.[7] From this, he goes on to argue that what he calls a blind faith and blind obedience are morally wrong. It is very difficult to argue against this line of thinking. Certainly, one of the self-authen-

7.   Don Cupitt, *Taking Leave of God*, 1980, London, SCM Press, p. ix.

ticating claims of the Gospel, ethically as much as any other way, would have to be that it somehow makes sense of itself, or that in Cupitt's terminology it is 'intrinsically good'. We are of course caught in something of a chicken and egg puzzle, for if God is real and not a cipher, then some part of basic human capability (obtainable from God at some stage if not actually 'built-in' to the individual by him) will be the individual's power of discernment as to what is, and what is not, 'intrinsically good', some kind of moral metering within. That there is a degree of the chicken and egg riddle about this question should not make it necessarily foolish to think of an objective God behind moral judgements.

The second revisit to Cupitt is to the conclusion of *The Last Philosophy* (which has in fact proved not to be the last philosophy of the author). In writing of Kingdom theology as something which will not give us external help and support but which will return us to ourselves, he recalls the story of the painter Henri Matisse who when, in old age, was asked if he believed in God, replied 'Yes, when I'm working'. Cupitt concludes by observing that looking at his work, one knows what he meant – 'Piety, not as patient submission and devotion, but as the production of joy' .[7] The phrase 'the production of joy' is evocative of much that has to do with goodness (and enchantment) and one certainly cannot disagree with a concept left floating there somewhere by Cupitt, that God is, when we engage with him and work with him.

Where I might wish us to go further than Cupitt (or perhaps, Matisse) is in suggesting that whereas God certainly 'is' for us, when we engage with him, that does not necessarily mean that he is *only* when we happen to be involving ourselves with him.

7.  Don Cupitt, *The Last Philosophy*, 1995, London, SCM Press, p.132.

# 9

## Wrestling Simone

When Simone Weil died in Kent in 1943, the verdict at her inquest was that of suicide. She had died of voluntary starvation. It was a poignant but somehow characteristic end to the short and often tormented life of a young woman, born into a French Jewish family of agnostic leanings in 1909 and dying an unbaptised and extremely unorthodox adherent of Christianity thirty-four years later.

Her reasons for refusing Baptism are the key to so much of her thinking. For her, so many things that she loved and would not reject were outside the Church, but she was certain that they were things which God loved, as otherwise he would not have given them existence.[1] And she could not bring herself to be separated from the multitude of unbelievers. Above all, she would not be adopted into a circle, 'to live among people who say "we" and to be part of an "us"'. Simone Weil was undoubtedly the quintessential warrior in our no-man's land. She carried her convictions to the point of refusing the comfort of belonging to the Church, as through her life she had struggled with the exigencies of apparent contradiction and certain paradox in her pursuit of God. As she once commented to a friend, the greatest disaster of all is to wrestle with God and not be beaten.[2]

A crucial aspect of her development in thought was her belief that contradiction is itself an essential criterion for reality. A mathematician and philosopher of undoubted brilliance, Weil also engaged with political life, embraced communism for a short time, and worked as an unskilled

1. Simone Weil, *Waiting on God*, 1951, London, Routledge & Kegan Paul, p. 26.
2. Richard Rees, *Simone Weil*, 1966, Oxford, Oxford University Press, p. 145.

labourer in factories and on farms. Her involvement in poli-
tics made her posit inherent contradictions in schemes for
social improvement. So, she would argue, having many children is an expression of true love, but the over-population of
a country is an evil; improving material conditions of a
country is clearly laudable, but concomitant with this will be
the loss of the country's soul. She concluded therefore that it
is only imaginary good things that do have not inherent
contradiction.

This, she goes on to argue, can be translated into the
human relationship with God. God gives himself to humankind either as powerful or as perfect. It is for us to choose
which he is. But it is in her understanding of the Incarnation
and especially of the cross that her powerful sense of a
fundamental paradox within truth becomes most apparent.

It explains at least some of Simone Weil's thought if we
review, however briefly, the catalysts which led her to her
tentative but deeply provocative grasp of Christ. She had
three initial encounters with Christianity, all of them liturgi-
cal or ecclesiastical. [3] The first was in Portugal, when the sight
of a procession to the ships on a patronal festival gave her the
strange sense that Christianity was somehow the religion of
slaves. The second was when, on a visit to the chapel of St
Francis in Assisi, she found herself with a sudden, inexplicable
impulse to pray. The third was attending Holy Week and
Easter liturgies in Solesmes. But she also attributed a major
role in her pilgrimage to reading George Herbert's famous
poem *Love bade me welcome*. As she said in a letter, 'I thought I
was only reciting a beautiful poem, but unknown to me, it was
a prayer.' [4]

---

3.  *Waiting on God*, p 20
4.  Simone Weil, *Seventy Letters*, trans. Richard Rees, London, Routledge and
    Kegan Paul, p. 142.

Love bade me welcome. Yet my soul drew back.
  Guiltie of dust and sinne.
But quick-eye'd Love, observing me grow slack
  From my first entrance in,
Drew nearer to me, sweetly questioning,
  If I lacked any thing.

A guest, I answer'd, worthy to be here:
  Love said, You shall be he.
I the unkinde, ungratefull? Ah, my deare,
  I cannot look on thee.
Love took my hand, and smiling did reply,
  Who made the eyes but I?

Truth, Lord, but I have marr'd them: let my shame
  Go where it doth deserve.
And know you not, sayes Love, who bore the blame?
  My dear, then I will serve,
You must sit down, sayes Love, and taste my meat
  So I did sit and eat.

It is certainly be an over-simplification to suggest that these incidents are the key to understanding all of Weil's subsequent theophany, but it is equally certain that they provide an invaluable backcloth. Simone de Beauvoir who had, interestingly if incidentally, been a friend and contemporary of Weil at university (and who had been beaten by Weil in the university examinations in philosophy) recalled Weil as a student weeping on hearing that a terrible famine had broken out in China. Beauvoir wrote that she envied Weil having the depth of care that could reach right across the world.

Simone Weil had indeed an amazing capacity for compassion. She truly believed, well in advance of modern liberation theology, that human beings are so created that those who crush others feel nothing; it is the person crushed who feels what is happening. She argued that unless one has placed oneself on the side of the oppressed, to feel with them, one cannot understand the reality of their situation. This goes a long way to explaining the remarkable way in which she came to link a creation-theology with a theology of the Incarnation, and theology itself with a pattern of discipleship.

But yet there was always, for her, a brooding sense of ambiguity and paradox, even of direct contradiction. God, she argues, created the universe but does not, in the main, command it – although he has the power to do so. Instead, two subordinate powers are permitted to control much of what goes on within creation. The first is a blind necessity which attaches to matter (including what she terms 'the psychic matter of the soul') and the other is the autonomy which is essential to thinking beings.

By loving those around us, we emulate a divine love which created us and all those whom we encounter. And by loving also the order of the world, we imitate the divine love which made the creation to which we also belong by nature. But God has also given to humanity an imaginary divinity, so that humanity may strip itself of this imaginary divinity just as Christ emptied himself of his real divinity. Herein lies the crisis. For the coming together of the divine and the human inevitably calls out for punishment. Reaching back into mythology, Weil recalls Prometheus who was destroyed for loving humanity too much, but also Hippolytus who was destroyed for being loved too much by the gods. So it follows that in Christ there must be a cataclysm. The function of such mediation itself demands a catastrophe: 'We cannot conceive of a descent of God towards man or the ascent of man towards God without a tearing asunder.' [5] Hence the cross.

The cross of Christ now relates to humanity, and to humanity's own relationship with creation, in what she discerns

---

5. Simone Weil, *Gravity and Grace*, 1952, London, Routledge and Kegan Paul, p. 81.

as the divine demand that men and women empty themselves of the imaginary divinity with which they have been invested. So, she writes, the road of discipleship is the denial of that illusory divinity. It is the renunciation of self as the centre of the world in imagination; it is the understanding of all other points in the world as equally centres; and it is the acceptance that the true centre of existence is outside the created world. It is discipleship because it is an acknowledgement of, and consent to, the rule of mechanical activity in matter, but equally an acknowledgement of, and consent to, free choice at the centre of each soul. Such consent, for Weil, is love itself.

In this line of thinking, she avoids the dangers of a crude dualism. She would never have claimed that her theology was wholly distinctive, but her mode of communicating it is compelling and utterly consonant with the dislocation and ambivalence which characterises her life and thought. Even the manner of her death was of a piece with her thinking. In the relative security of the England of 1942, she refused to eat more than would have been available to those on rations in occupied France. Having contracted an infection of the lung, she still refused to eat properly, and her general weak condition meant that, from a medical perspective, she died totally unnecessarily. Seven people attended her funeral.

André Gide described her as the patron saint of all outsiders. This role as the outsider – and it was in many respects a self-appointed role – meant that her relationship with collectivism, the corporate in Christian discipleship, was inevitably contentious and (it must be admitted) not wholly sustainable. Weil wrote compellingly of a theology of person-hood and community in terms of two modes of God-language. What she had to say was not particularly original but she conveys it with characteristic thrust. The two God-languages are, she suggests, made up of the same words but totally incomprehensible to one another. The Comforter, the spirit of truth, speaks

in one or other of the languages as circumstances demand.
The first is the collective language, spoken to the community.
The second is the personal language, spoken to the individual. She suggests that by the necessity of their nature, the
languages are totally different. There must always be an
unbridgeable gap between, as she puts it, the language of the
market place and the market of the wedding chamber.[6]
Where this road takes her, however, is to a refusal to relate to
the collective, *qua* collective. In one of her letters on Baptism
she wrote:

> I love God, Christ and the Catholic faith as much as it is
> possible for so miserably inadequate a creature to love
> them. I love the saints through their writings and what is
> told of their lives – apart from some who it is impossible
> to love fully or to consider as saints.
>
> I love the six or seven Catholics of genuine spirituality
> whom chance has led me to meet in the course of my life.
> I love the Catholic liturgy, hymns, architecture, rites and
> ceremonies. But I have not the slightest love for the
> Church in the strict sense of the word, apart from its
> relation to all these things that I do love.[7]

It seems churlish in the extreme to suggest that there was
a streak of self-indulgence in anyone as clearly sincere about
self-renunciation as Weil. Yet it must be said that here she
allowed herself a luxury which she must have known could not
be enjoyed (if that is the correct word) by many. To hear the
collective God-language, and to appreciate the benefits and
effects of that language and yet refuse to enter into that
community is indeed a self-indulgence, and it is the less
worthy aspect of her sense of self-sacrifice in refusing Baptism
and so remaining, sacramentally at least, outside the commu-

6. *Waiting on God*, p. 30.
7. *Ibid*. p. 6.

nity of the Church. Here there seems to be a reluctance to bear the pain and to face the vulnerability of being within something which has been corrupted and compromised. Yet it is perfectly feasible to love the Church from within (while partly hating it), and still loving all that which is loveable and God-given and God-loved outside it.

In his biography of Michael Ramsey (Archbishop of Canterbury from 1961 until 1974), his Press Officer Michael De-La-Noy tells the story (which has since passed into folk-lore) of the genuinely saintly archbishop, being all but stranded on a overseas visit, due to a airport strike. He tells us that the Archbishop was totally unperturbed by this. Indeed he gave the impression of someone who had no particular desire to return to England then or ever. Arriving into Ramsey's bedroom to give him news on the progress of events, his press officer found stretched out on his bed repeating, almost as manta, 'I hate the Church of England, I hate the Church of England.'[8]

That story of Ramsey seems to me to show a perfectly proper and reasonable relationship with the Church-community. It has always seemed to me that it should have been within Simone Weil's capability to love the Church as the recipient of the collective God-language (and indeed the bearer of that language), while simultaneously finding it contemptible. But it must be said, in fairness to her, that anything that might be seen as escapism was abhorrent to her. Redemption and access to the transcendent could only be found in a life rooted in the everyday hurts of humanity. Glory for her could never be found only on a vertical access, and a mysticism which tried to remove itself from human affliction was an abomination to her. Yet she could not accept that the affliction of humanity could ever be divorced from the perfection of God, however

8. Michael De-La-Noy, *Michael Ramsey, A Portrait*, 1990, London, Collins, pp. 161-2.

self-contradictory that gulf might be. Indeed the contradiction almost gave it a certainty. It is, she believed, as wrong to retreat from the world in favour of the Absolute because this is a counterfeit mysticism, as it is to turn objects in the world into absolutes which is straightforward idolatry.

For all the lucidity and brilliance of her exposition of a theology of creation and cross, there is no doubt but that, on paper at least, Simone Weil was also prone to most of the heresies carefully expunged by the Church over centuries. She believed that Plato was of more value than the Old Testament; she had admiration for the Gnostic tendencies of the Cathars; she was in some respects more Hindu than Christian – one could continue for some time enumerating the aspects of the heterodox in her spirituality.

But she was a prophet. She was a fascinating individual of searching, brilliant and speculative intelligence who had the courage to roam and struggle in a no-man's land, so that authentic love for God and creation could advance. And she truly believed that 'if we love God while thinking he does not exist, he will manifest his existence'. [9]

9.  *Gravity and Grace*, p. 15.

# 10

# A Most Tremendous Tale?

The 'place' that believers and disbelievers accord to the Bible in their understanding of faith is not only the site of much discord and acrimony. It is also at the very heart of the question which the thinking Christian must level at the basis of his or her faith, 'But is it actually true?' Some extrinsic authority for the Bible in telling the tale of Christianity is surely crucial if we are to regard the tale itself as of continuing consequence.

In the first place, it clearly will not do to say that the Bible is true because it says its true, as biblical fundamentalists tend to do. This is at best a circular argument, and at worst a cowardly refusal to be rigorous or even honest, either spiritually or intellectually. The Bible must itself be assailable and vulnerable if it can be a bearer of the vulnerable God, and when we turn seriously to the question of an authority, other than one which the individual reader bestows on the Bible, we are indeed left in a vulnerable position.

What, if anything, makes the Bible different from any other book? Well over a century ago Benjamin Jowett was pilloried for his famous suggestion, in *Essays and Reviews*, that only when we read the Bible like any other book will we discover that it is different from any other book. If we do read the Bible like any other book, we may indeed find ourselves giving it a special status, but we must still question whether that individualist authority is enough. It must certainly 'make sense' to us, but it should also have some authority to which we may try to relate objectively.

We need to accept at the start of everything we might say about the Scriptures that the Bible is a human book about God. That does not thereby strip it of authority but it removes from it a false and dangerous supernaturalism with which it so often and so mistakenly invested.

A detailed history of how the separate books of the Bible were acknowledged to be the Bible (what is technically called the formation of the canon of Scripture) is beyond the requirements of this book, but some of the basics are important. If we know how the Bible became the Bible, we can then decide how we should think of it.

What was to be the Old Testament canon (from a Christian perspective) seems to have been decided late in the first century CE. It tends to be assumed that after the fall of Jerusalem, the rabbis under Johanan ben Zakkai fixed the canon of 'inspired' books, as far as the requirements of Jewish worship were concerned. This was ultimately taken into the Christian scheme of things and although some of the Reformed Churches, fifteen hundred years later, reduced the list (removing what they termed the Apocrypha), there matters remained. When it comes to the New Testament canon we are into the fourth century and Eusebius, before any proper standardisation of what was to be in and what was to be out becomes apparent. Books, for example, such as the Letter of James, or the Second Letter of Peter, had an extremely chequered career of inclusion within, and exclusion from, various canons before final acceptance. A series of synods at the end of the fourth centuries provided what might be called the final list.

All that this sketch does establish is that the Bible was not definitive from the outset. The experience of generations of the Jewish community in the case of what we call the Old Testament, and of the Christian community for the New Testament, established that certain sacred texts were recognisable as inspired. But we are speaking of the shared experience of community.

We may peel the onion a little further and recall that the

books within the Bible are themselves, in many cases, the product of the reflection and interpretation of generation upon generation of God-directed people and were undoubtedly added to and subtracted from, in the course of transition from spoken story to final written version of the story. As has therefore to be said repeatedly, the Bible is the book of the community, seeing within itself God revealed. The earliest generations of Christians were spiritually and intellectually persuaded that certain books were revealing God, bearing God. The importance of this should not be reduced to the mundane. One may with complete integrity speak of the Bible as 'the Word of God', revealing God with the decisive spiritual authority which also inspired centuries of reflection finally to recognise it as being 'inspired'.

A question which immediately follows is whether – if the Spirit of God is active in the Churches for all time – the canon of Scripture should ever have been closed. A rather prosaic answer has to be that the essence of the authority of the Bible for Christians is that all Christians can accept that authority. It may well be that other non-biblical individual books have 'done more' for individual Christians (or even entire Christian communities) than have some of the more obscure tracts of Scripture. But it is the recognition of the same Scripture throughout the entire Church as 'the Bible' which, logistically if for no other reason, could not be extended to any other piece of writing.

One has then to move on and ask whether one can adopt an *à la carte* attitude to Scripture, showing individual discrimination in what one will accept as authoritative, and in what one will not concede as of value. It is perhaps here more than anywhere else that the essential vulnerability of Christian discipleship is exposed. It can, however, be said with complete integrity that humility, and reverence for Scripture are not incompatible with an intelligent reading of a text which will

seek to delineate poetry from history, law code from homily,
and symbol from exhortation. If we turn what is symbol or
metaphor into history we do God no honour. The removal of
the Bible to a ghetto of mindlessness is idolatry of the worst
kind.

Karl Barth, in his monumental *Church Dogmatics*, explained
how the Bible can be seen truly as revelation, and yet never
become an object of idolatrous worship itself.[1] For Barth,
God's Word is at the centre of all Christian discipleship and
this Word must be seen always in dynamic rather than static
terms. It is never to be conceptualised as mere words or even
as statements of faith, but as an event, something which
actually takes place. God's Word is the event of God speaking
to human beings in Jesus Christ; that is what is truly to be
meant by God's revelation of himself to us. To make God's
word a static object (even as the Bible), which humanity can
anatomise, is to bring it under our control. God's Word
confronts us not as an object which we can master, but as the
ultimate Subject which masters us. God's Word is something
that happens to us – the event of God revealing himself to us
through Jesus Christ. It is not a manual of godly data but a
dynamic event which demands a response from us.

If we say that God's Word is the event of God speaking to us
and revealing himself to us through Jesus Christ, the Bible
then becomes the attestation of this revelation. Barth makes
it very clear that 'to attest is to point in a definite direction
beyond oneself to something else. Attestation is, therefore,
the service of this something else, in which the witness answers
for the truth of this something else'.

He goes on to show how it is the written Word of God which
makes possible the proclaimed Word of God today. The
Church today, through the proclaimed Word, attests to and

---

1. What follows below is derived from Volume 1, part I, section 4, of Barth's
   *Church Dogmatics*, 1960, Edinburgh, T & T Clark.

bears witness to the revealed Word. This proclamation is to be based on the written Word, the Bible. The Church has no right to preach anything else.

And so, in Barth's understanding, the written Word and the proclaimed Word are not in themselves revelation, but are human language pointing to God's revelation of himself. As human words, they are finite and inadequate, but they become the Word of God when he chooses to speak to us through them. In other words, the written Word and the proclaimed Word, albeit of God's choosing and God's grace, actually become that to which they bear witness – God speaking to us in Jesus Christ. Barth is very clear that the Bible must always be understood as at the service of the Word:

> Why and in what respect does the Biblical witness possess authority? In that it claims no authority for itself, that its witness amounts to letting the Something else be the authority, itself and of its own agency. Therefore we do the Bible a poor honour, and one unwelcome to itself, when we directly identify it with this Something else, with revelation itself. [2]

One of the most moving accounts in literature of the impact of how the reading of the Bible becomes revelation is in Dostoevsky's *Crime and Punishment*. Raskolnikov, the tormented murderer at the centre of the narrative, visits Sonya, the strange and almost saintly prostitute who eventually begins the process of his redemption by her love for him. Sonya makes Raskolnikov read the section of John's Gospel where Lazarus is raised from the dead. Nothing happens to Raskolnikov in any dramatic fashion. Yet, in some mysterious way, that intensely moving event marks the beginning of his redemption. [3]

2. *Ibid.* p. 126
3. Dostoevsky, *Crime and Punishment* trans. Jessie Coulson , 1980, Oxford, Oxford University Press, pp. 313 ff

The Jewish philosopher Martin Buber paid Christians a tremendous compliment when he suggested that for Jews the Book is the sanctuary, whereas for Christians it is the vestibule. Sadly, the compliment has not been accepted by nearly enough Christians. Buber believed that we, Jews and Christians, should live together in the space the Bible provides, and listen to the voice that speaks in it. The thinking believer must accept this space, but it is also a vulnerable and exposed space where people will attack far more readily than they will listen.

Indeed, it is another no-man's land between three opposing formations of warriors. There are those who will use the Bible only as a convenient source for carefully selected extracts that will support the viewpoint they would wish to hold anyhow. There are also those who believe that the Bible requires their personal expertise in bowdlerisation to be pure and undefiled. And, finally, there are those who, when they open the Bible, ignore the fact that there is a command within that they worship God, at least in part, with their minds. Any no-man's land between three sets of trenches is indeed an unenviable location!

The place of the Bible among other sacred texts which have also fulfilled the criteria of 'reception' within other faith-communities raises difficulties for many. May one say logically that the Christian Bible has any claims to superiority over the Koran or the Bhagavad-Gita which have also been received as bearing God by other communities who seek God? Behind this question lies a deeper question over the exclusiveness of Christian claims to be 'right'. It is here that the notion of engagement, more fully discussed in the final chapter, must be invoked.

It is certainly possible to take an eclectic approach to religion, using religion as a spiritual *smorgasbord* with a personal selection of titbits from a variety of religions; but that is to use religion as a hobby. Somewhere there has to be a movement from the dilettante to the committed, to the totally engaged. One may legitimately say 'This is right for me and because I am so convinced of its rightness, I want to convince others of its rightness'. Indeed if we are thoroughly enthused by anything – a sport, a piece of music, or a beautiful view – we will inevitably want to involve others in our enthusiasm and convince them of its value. Sadly, this trait is rarely noticeable in adherents of the main stream Christian traditions in western society. But an overriding enthusiasm which wishes to convince others does not allow us to assume that God will automatically wish to punish those who are not convinced by what we believe to be a supreme rightness. That is, in every sense, his business and not ours.

The areas of the New Testament which have, when considered afresh by radical or liberal thinkers, most attracted the attention of outraged conservatives, both biblical and ecclesiastical, have been (literally for centuries) the virgin birth of Jesus and his resurrection. There have been many great Christians, among them William Temple, whose acceptability to the Church was seriously questioned because of their own questioning on virgin birth and resurrection. As so often, orthodoxy has had little to do with belief, and a great deal more to do with vocabulary.

If we take a proverbial step back and ask what may be the real significance of what is being said, whether in the New Testament or the ancient credal statements of the Church, the physiological details of either the birth or the resurrection are of little importance. If one can affirm that in some mysterious but not irrational way, Jesus Christ was the fullness of human-ness but also the fullness of divine-ness in a decisive and unique way, then a description of his birth which predicates this uniqueness is not an extract from a biological textbook. In a sense, the obstetrics and gynaecology are not what is significant or interesting. It is the presentation of Christ as unique in human-ness and and in divine-ness that matters.

Similarly with the resurrection. It is not medical aspects of recusitation which should fascinate. It is the fact that whatever happened on the first Easter morning (which, in my own view, must have been something objective rather than a subjective spiritual re-awakening of the disciples in order to have had the effect it did), so galvanised the followers of Christ that they were utterly transformed and stayed transformed. If God is God, then he could certainly have 'produced' a virgin-birth and a bodily resurrection. The physiology is not of the slightest importance or interest, in contrast to the eternal significance of the Incarnation and the Resurrection. One of the sad degradations to which the Church has subjected the Gospel has been a concern to turn trees into totem poles and to neglect the true glory of the spiritual wood.

The Christian creeds, on the other hand, look also at wood, or at least at some types of wood. As with the formation of the canon of the Bible, the creeds developed over centuries, although with even greater controversy and hostility on all sides. The creeds were designed to delineate the borders of what was perceived as the true Christian faith, and to act as an exclusion order on those whose Christian faith, however sincere, did not conform. The historical creeds have continued to be the plumb-line for orthodox Christian belief. And they have not ceased to be a focus of controversy.

The so-called Athanasian Creed, particularly as its later text heaped damnation on those who could not, or would not, subscribe to its extraordinarily complex, and at times barely comprehensible explication of Trinitarian and Christological orthodoxy, was the cause of much polemic and debate in the nineteenth century. In the twentieth century it seems to have been given the status of a slightly senile relation, acknowledged as part of the family, but not woken unnecessarily, as prone to nastiness when aroused.

What is immediately apparent about the creeds is first, that the heresies they seek to vanquish have survived remarkably well. There are still to be found, for example, countless Arians who give to Jesus Christ a divinity slightly subordinate to that of the Father. The difference is that they are now happily within the Church and do not know what Arianism means. The second feature is that the language of the creeds is that of Greek philosophy. It is not a mode of thought or expression which is understood fully today, except by experts in university libraries. If we were to write creeds today, they would be vastly different, both in language and in the concerns addressed. The creeds should, nevertheless, be taken both seriously and intelligently. But we should hold, in some form of tension, the function of the historical creeds in opposing distortions, with their setting in cultures and thought patterns totally different to ours.

In this context of doing theology, I believe that much that is interesting (and much that is trivial) has over the centuries centred on the theological 'method', when approaching any theological question, of seeking to balance three complementary strands: Scripture, tradition, and reason – Scripture as the revelation of God; tradition as the seeking by means of historical experience (the past and the present) to interpret the present; and reason as the contemporaneous insights of knowledge, conscience and intelligence, the three working in a creative tension.

There is danger in any approach which would treat these three strands as if they could actually be separated to any degree. As we have already suggested, the Scriptures are themselves the product of a Christian tradition of several centuries duration which compiled, nurtured, and ultimately selected the books which have become the Scriptures. What is within the Bible is, therefore, itself tradition if we understand tradition in any natural sense. Similarly, any reading of

the Scriptures is not a neutral or neutered undertaking.
Metaphorically, we read the Bible through spectacles, tinted
in part by what life has made us as individuals, but also by the
way in which we have already been conditioned, in other
words by the culture or tradition of which we are part. When,
as a northern European, I read the Bible, it is not in the same
way as a north American or as any one of several African
traditions. We bring subliminally to our reading, from first
glance to intensive study, something of the culture and
tradition which has brought us to reading the Bible in the first
place. It goes without saying that the component of reason is
moulded by both Scripture and tradition, and it is also an
unrecognised intrusion into our reading of the Bible and our
meditating upon the tradition which has nurtured us. The
concept of the three strands is useful only when we find a
better terminology than 'strands'.

Every Christian employs Scripture, tradition and reason in
some mode. Where the value of the method comes is when we
admit that whenever we are consciously veering towards any
of the poles, Scripture, tradition or reason alone, we are
axiomatically wrong. The technical term *symbiosis*, which
means that all the components require each other in order to
continue, is too bland and contented to convey the vulnerability and passion that should be part of the exploration. The
danger for even the most lucid of theological explications is
that decorum becomes the most important ingredient. For, as
Buber would remind us, no 'tradition' is ever more than a
vestibule.

One of the best-known images in this regard is that used by
George Herbert in a poem which has become a much-loved
hymn:

> A man who looks on glass
> On it may stay his eye;
> Or, if he pleaseth, through it pass,
> And then the heaven espy.[4]

It becomes too easy for the tradition, or the text, or even the particular Christian denomination to become the end result of the search for an authentic Christian discipleship. There may be a great deal of beauty and fulfilment to be found in these tools for finding truth. They have to remain tools, or they become idolatrous.

To update Herbert's imagery a little, the computer, microscope or telescope may easily and pleasantly become toys in themselves rather than the means to produce or to discover. We may be very proud of our latest computer, microscope or telescope, but if we never get beyond the point of bragging about its ability or potential, little is gained. So with the spiritual instruments we use. We are guilty of the grossest immaturity if we do not ask others what they have discovered through their clever gadgets and instruments as well.

4. George Herbert, *The Complete English Poems*, 1991, Harmondsworth, Penguin Books.

# 11

# Truth But Not as We Know It

Much of what has been said thus far arrives, from various directions, at the conclusion that the pursuit of truth, or God, or both, will always be disturbing. Elusiveness is part of the reality of authentic believing. And untidiness is equally a dimension of any truth which is more than conceptual.

In a whimsical piece of imagery in his novel *Niebla*, Unamuno rather obliquely compares an umbrella with the pursuit of truth. One of the characters, Augusto, hates having to open his umbrella because when it is not in use, it is 'so elegant, so slim, folded in its case'. Indeed for him a closed umbrella is as elegant as an open umbrella is ugly.[1] Unamuno suggests that it is an unfortunate aspect of having to make use of things that this inevitably brings out their unattractive characteristics. Truth unused can be extremely elegant and even plausible. When it is put to practical purposes, it becomes unwieldy and far less aesthetically pleasing.

It is a corollary of this that there will always be a vulnerability in belief and, for truth to live, there must also be a genuine commitment to the pursuit of it. But if we accept that this untidiness, vulnerability, elusiveness and commitment are the *sine qua non* for a faith that is more than a cardboard cut-out imitation, can we move into this morass without separating ourselves from what we are as intelligent beings?

Camus, who has entered directly (and at other times tangentially) into much of what has discussed in the preceding chapters, believed, as has been noted, that this place between the untidinesses and the irrationality of existence

---

1. Translation of this section – ed. José Rubin Garcia and M A Zeitlin, *Unamuno – Creation and Creator*, 1967, University of California Press 1967). Leon Livingstone, 'The novel as self-creation' p. 92

and a craving for clarity and meaning behind existence was an essential absurdity which is, for all our posturing and writhing, all there is in reality to being a human. In a passionate chapter in *The Myth of Sisyphus* [2] he also vented his impatience with the existentialists who slotted God into this gap between all that defies rationality, on the one hand, and the human demands for rationality, on the other. He berated the Russian philosopher Leon Chestov in particular, suggesting that when Chestov discovered the essential absurdity of the all existence, instead of saying 'This is absurd', he says 'This is God'.

Camus' treatment of the doyen of Christian existentialism, Søren Kierkegaard, was, if anything, even more caustic. He was convinced that the demand of Kierkegaard that, on facing the paradox and even the scandal of Christianity, we can only take a 'leap' in faith, was the suicide of the intellect. Camus speaks vehemently of Kierkegaard's mutilation of the soul in order to balance the mutilation accepted in regard to the absurd. He could come only to the conclusion that the absurd does not lead to God. Camus very explicitly refused to say that the absurd excludes God, and he made the extraordinarily theological comment that 'the absurd is sin without God'.

And yet (perhaps even despite himself) there is, elsewhere in his writings, some sort of minimalist resolution for Camus, even what he calls a consummation to the struggle. In the conclusion of what is probably his most famous book, *The Outsider* (more correctly *The Stranger*), the central character Meursault, awaiting execution for a murder he may well not have committed, having fought for his non-faith with the bland prison chaplain, finds that peace arrives so that 'all may be consummated'. [3] Despite the clear and intentional parallel with the words of Christ on the cross, 'It is finished / consum-

2. Albert Camus, *The Myth of Sisyphus*, trans. Justin O'Brien, 1975, Harmondsworth, Penguin Books, 'Philosophical Suicide', pp. 32-51.
3. Albert Camus, *The Outsider*, trans. Joseph Laredo, 1982, Harmondsworth, Penguin Books, p. 117.

mated', this is no final last-minute surrender to the truth of the claims of Christianity. It is, in that elusiveness so character-istic of Camus, a glimmer of something which harmonises, even if it is in his words only 'the tender indifference of the universe'. Camus was as capable as Kierkegaard of exulting in paradox.

If we wish to move beyond Kierkegaard, who argued that truth is subjectivity (and hence that subjective sincerity is a genuine criterion of truth), and to say that for truth to be real it must possess more than subjectivity even it cannot possess all the implacable objectivity we might wish it to have, how much further can we proceed?

Can further progress be made only at the cost of all rationality? Unamuno would have replied in the negative. He could not accept the blanket either/or leap of faith de-manded by Kierkegaard. Similarly, although Unamuno might admire Pascal, he was temperamentally incapable of accept-ing the cool detachment in the latter's famous suggestion that Christianity was sufficiently plausible as to make it worth the wager of one's commitment, in that one lost nothing if it turned out to be untrue, and gained everything if it all turned out to be true. For Unamuno, belief without passion and commitment was not belief. For him, there had to be both passion in belief and also a personal requirement to believe, but for him this belief might then be reasonably and objec-tively validated through the person of Christ and through history. [4]

If we follow broadly the approach of Unamuno and say that a totally subjective faith is intellectual nonsense, and a totally objective faith can never be more than a chimera, can we make anything of the place of passion as the space in between,

---

4. Miguel de Unamuno, *The Agony of Christianity and Essays on Faith*, trans. Anthony Kerrigan, 1974, London, Routledge and Kegan Paul, 'My Reli-gion', pp. 209-217.

as our no-man's land? Hans Urs Von Balthasar employs the rather different imagery of the attempted creation of a bridge. [5] He suggests that the idea of God remains in itself uncompletable for humanity. There are two points of departure in the search – the purely philosophical, and the experiential world of religion. But they cannot create a span which will meet the other. Instead of consigning this gap to the realm of the absurd, Balthasar argues that the only possibility of bridging the gap is in the exercise of love in community. He writes elsewhere of the tension between the unknowable God, the God in unapproachable light of 1 Timothy and the God who can be approached, as the writer of the Epistle to the Ephesians put it, in boldness and confidence. So, Balthasar urges that Christians today must be capable of withstanding the tension which is contained within these statements of the transcendence and the immanence of God. On the one hand, they must abandon every effort to penetrate into the hidden and free being of God with 'unbaptised reason'; and on the other, they must neglect no path which God himself offers humankind into the mystery of his eternal love.

Balthasar believes that the individual who can come to acknowledge God will accept the terrifying limitations of humanity and so be drawn beyond himself. 'Man must suffocate through man if, in this everlasting meeting with himself which makes up his daily life, he meets no one else save man, no matter whether he meets himself in solitude or in community, in solitary community or in the crowds of traffic in the road ... ' Humanity, Balthasar concludes, must encounter God in the love for brother or sister, and there must be the 'breath of infinity' in the stirring of this love. Such a love must be known to come from God and as returning to God. [6]

5. Ed. Medard Kehl and Werner Löser, *The Von Balthasar Reader*, trans. Robert J Daly and Fred Lawrence, 1982, Edinburgh, T & T Clark, p. 101.
6. Hans Urs Von Balthasar, *Science, Religion and Christianity*, 1958, London Burns and Oates, 'The Sacrament of the Brother', p. 142 ff.

Developing Balthasar's position, we may say that the gap
between the indications that there possibly is a God and the
innate human desire for God can only be bridged in the
working out of love. The passive absurd is replaced by the
action of love for others. If we return briefly to *The Plague*, it
is this love in action which explains Rieux the doctor, and
which creates the strange truce between him and the priest
Paneloux.[7] For an understanding of the pain and ambiguity of
that place between the trenches we must turn to Camus rather
than Balthasar for insight.

There must, underneath all else, be the continuing demand for truth. To be afraid of truth, to be afraid to change
ones' ideas is, in the poet Blake's phrase only 'to breed reptiles
in the mind'. For, as Unamuno saw, 'the only perfect homage
that can be rendered to God is the homage of truth. The
Kingdom of God, whose advent is mechanically exhorted
every day by millions of tongues defiled by lies, is none other
than the Kingdom of truth'.[8] Unamuno would not have been
the man he was if he had been able to resist carrying this
insight through to the point of paradox and dislocation, a
highly appropriate displacement if we retain in our mind the
terrifying image of no-man's land.

> Blessed are the pure in heart for they shall see God! Tell
> your truth to God always and God will tell you His. And
> you will see God and die. For the scriptures say that
> whoever sees God shall die. And that is the best that can
> happen in a world of lies: to die of seeing the Truth.[9]

That is indeed, in the familiar phrase of *Star Trek*, 'truth but
not as we know it … ' Or may wish to know it.

---

7.  See above, pp. 46-48.
8.  Miguel de Unamuno, *The Agony of Christianity and Essays on Faith*, 'What is
    truth?', p 168.
9.  *Ibid.* p. 184.